Can taking emotion to work really enhance
demonstrated by corporate coach and vetera
as she explores 16 fundamental emotional skills vital for workplace success
using Dr. Reuven Bar-On's proven model of emotional intelligence in Emotion
at Work. This is a must-read book for C-suite executives who want insider tips
to skyrocket their careers and motivate their teams to perform at their peak.
Roberta is spot-on!

Craig Palubliak, President
Optim Group

Skilled psychotherapist Roberta Moore expertly explains how taking emotion
to work can be the make-or-break difference that takes you from being stuck in
less-than-optimal performance to stellar success – and professional brilliance.
Her suggestions are on-point with helping managers improve their leadership
skills from day one. Spend one hour with Roberta and you too can experience
what I have come to enjoy in our professional dealings.

Rod Cooper, Founder and Owner
RKCC Coaching and Speaking LLC

Many people choose to live a life of quiet desperation not knowing what causes
them to behave in certain ways and not realizing how that impacts their re-
lationships. I invite you to engage in the purposeful and challenging work of
self-exploration discussed in this book. The journey isn't always easy, but the
reward is great – a happier, more productive life filled with better personal
and professional relationships.

Gerard M. Hempstead CPA, CFP®, Managing Partner
Northwestern Mutual – St. Louis

I wish I had read this book as I grew my entrepreneurial business from start to
succession over 24 years. Understanding the 16 fundamental emotional skills
would have brought welcome additional research and experience foundations
as I led and motivated my team.

Roberta Moore willingly shares her own personal challenges, as well as com-
pelling composite stories from years in psychological practice and business
management. Read the book for a valuable overview of the emotional intelli-
gence model; complete the detailed exercises to get the full benefit of her work.

Cathy Dunkin, Lecturer in Management
Olin Business School – Washington University in St. Louis

Roberta Moore is a skilled psychotherapist and coach from whom I've greatly benefited. Roberta used her expertise in emotional intelligence to help me become a better leader and person both inside and outside the workplace. I hope everyone who reads this book will benefit as much as I did from Roberta's practical knowledge and emotional intelligence expertise.

Peter J Daneels, Residential Director
Mooseheart Child & City School

Roberta Moore is committed to whatever she takes on. I work with her in in her volunteer capacity in various areas of the St Louis entrepreneurial community. She enthusiastically takes on projects and works them intensely until they are completed. We have served on committees and boards together, and she impresses everyone with her drive, her truly pleasant manner and her outstanding results.

Joe Soraghan, Attorney
Danna McKitrick P

Roberta, your presentation was a big hit with my class—they felt your sincerity, warmth, and persistence in your comments. We all look forward to your book.

James F O'Donnell III, Senior Partner
O'DONNELL CAPITAL COMPANY, LLC

A must read for any leader, team or individual who wants to enhance and even propel to the next level of workplace performance and career. Roberta Moore's eloquent style and extensive experience encourages the reader to do self-exploration of the 16 fundamental emotional skills vital for workplace success. Examples of real situations interwoven with her personal story and balanced approach engages the reader to follow the proven model of Dr. Reuven Bar-On regarding emotional intelligence. Benefits from reading this book are very real and relevant for personal and work-place success.

Peggy Northcott, Managing Partner
Capital Performance

Emotion at Work

Unleashing the Secret Power
of Emotional Intelligence

Roberta Ann Moore

Conscious Choices Corporation, St. Louis, Missouri

Emotion at Work:
Unleashing the Secret Power of Emotional Intelligence

ISBN-13: 978-1985879607
ISBN-10: 1985879603

Conscious Choices Corporation St. Louis, Missouri

Contents

I dedicate this book to my husband, Scott Schenck,
for his unwavering faith and support of me.

Acknowledgments

I want to thank the following people and companies for inspiring and encouraging me to get this book into the world: Gerard Hempstead, Yemi Akande, Dr.Keith Parker, Dr. Dana Ackley, Doug McKinley, Korrel Kanoy, Christy Oldani, Cathy Davis, Craig Palubiak, Tim Sansone, Brandon Dempsey, Meridith Elliott Powell, Cindy McDaniel, Debi Corrie and my Vistage Group.

In addition: Nicole Rollender, the best editor I could have! She made me sound so much better than I would otherwise; and Casaundra Bennett, for having the magic touch that sparked my writing. I also thank my clients, the ultimate inspiration for the character composites in this volume.

Introduction: Why I Wrote This Book

As I walked through the door of Chelsea's Tearoom in Asheville, North Carolina, it was like stepping back into old England: chintz tablecloths and carnations on the tables, and oil paintings of lush, flowered landscapes. Whenever I visited Chelsea's, I was transported out of western North Carolina into my own version of heaven: tea served in genuine British red-floral teapots, along with the aromas of fresh tea, muffins, and three dessert cakes.

On this particular visit, a chilly January Saturday, I was alone at my table, looking out into an intimate courtyard. Usually, my husband, Scott, came with me, since it was our favorite weekend lunch spot. He had already relocated to St. Louis to start his new job, though, and I was staying on in Hendersonville, North Carolina, for a few more months before I'd join him.

While waiting for my chicken Cobb salad, I pulled out reading material from my bag – the Multi-Health Systems (MHS) catalog of psychological assessments, which had arrived one day in my mailbox. As I opened the catalog, I felt chills when I saw an ad for the Emotional Quotient Inventory (EQ-i 2.0) assessment tool, which measures emotional intelligence.

MHS defines emotional intelligence as a "set of emotional and social skills that influence the way we perceive and express ourselves, develop and maintain social relationships, cope with challenges, and use emotional information in an effective and meaningful way." This training tool is often used by businesses for employee development, recruitment and retention.

The EQ-i 2.0 assessment is based on the work of Dr. Reuven Bar-On, a psychologist and one of the world's leading researchers and theorists in emotional intelligence. The Bar-On Model of Emotional Intelligence comprises 16 skills, grouped into five composites, which anyone can learn in order to raise his or her level of emotional intelligence – leading to a happier and more productive life.

The chills I experienced that morning weren't from fear, but rather, excitement. I recalled a quick-read talk paper based on Daniel Goleman's book, *Emotional Intelligence: Why It Can Matter More Than IQ*, that St. Louis-based therapist Laura Batchelor had written for me. Laura was the first therapist I worked with who taught me emotional intelligence skills. She gifted me with this summary paper when I first left St. Louis years earlier to move to the Carolinas.

I had re-read Laura's paper numerous times, highlighting important sections like: "The key ability of emotional skills is governing emotional responses, that is, controlling the impulse rather than allowing the emotion to control you, and then formulating an acceptable and effective feeling response." And this important section asserting that just as we have toes and fingers and eyes, we also have feelings (like mad, sad and glad), and just as we control our body parts, we also need to master our feelings, otherwise, "If you aren't the conscious director of these physical feelings, you're the unconscious passenger in them. You're being victimized by them. You're not directing mad, sad, glad and fear as you've learned to direct your arms, eyes, toes and legs."

In that aha moment, I interpreted my visceral reaction to the EQ-i 2.0 ad as a sure sign I needed to take action. This was a true pivotal moment: Right then and there, I pulled out my laptop and found an upcoming certification class in Raleigh, North Carolina, in March.

"This is perfect timing," I thought. I could complete my certification as I was finishing my stay in Hendersonville right before I moved to St. Louis in April, to join my husband. I'd have my certificate in hand, ready to work with executive and professional clients when I arrived. I was very, very excited.

I had been searching for a new structure, a new model that would combine my therapeutic expertise with my business background – the EQ-i 2.0 was one I could embrace. After more than a decade into my work as a clinical therapist, I was feeling restless, though it certainly wasn't the clients or the work. I felt split: I had a business background (I had been in the financial industry for 18 years before I opened my therapy practice), sitting alongside my psychology mindset and therapy training.

For a while, I'd been searching for a way to integrate these two parts of myself, to feel whole again. When I left the business world, I felt

I had abandoned a part of myself, along with a whole set of valuable skills. I wanted that part of myself back again! Something was urging me on, encouraging me to move beyond my comfort zone. For sure, at that time, I was comfortable with a full therapy practice and a good number of long-term clients.

However, there was more. I had begun to notice that my clients who began working with me to unravel issues related to their families and personal lives inevitably began to talk about their work lives. It became clear that the skills they needed to create happy and fluid home lives were the same skills that would boost their happiness and contentment at work. Aha again! If I could show my professional clients how to employ a psychological approach in the workplace, without the stigma sometimes attached to that, I could use both my hard and soft skillsets, while also better serving my clients. When I spotted the EQ-i 2.0 assessment training ad, I realized I had found a way to make a real difference in my clients' lives.

Closer to home, there were personal reasons why I was attracted to working with emotional intelligence. As I thought about the paper Laura Batchelor had given me, she often stressed the importance of integrity: being in integrity with oneself, acting with integrity and offering integrity to others. As a young woman, when I began to act as completely as possible out of integrity, my life changed. First of all, I developed a relationship with myself: I began to be true to my inner wisdom. I listened to her messages and honored them in the form of action. When I acted in alignment in that manner, my self-confidence shot up. When I acted outside of that integrity, even in what some might consider a minor way, I felt I had let myself down.

Living in integrity with myself was the first step toward building more authentic relationships with others. As a young adult, I paid more attention to things like showing up early for meetings, paying my bills on time, keeping my home clean, preparing healthy meals for myself, following through on promises I had made and meeting work deadlines. What I didn't realize then was that I was building the practice of self-regard, the skill at the foundation of the other emotional intelligence skills. Before long, my dedication to this new way of life paid off big-time: I got a much better job and through that new company, I met and married my husband.

Now, let me take you back even farther. I grew up in an intensely critical household. Daily, I heard: "You're crazy," "You don't see things clearly," "You don't know what you're talking about" and "You've got it all wrong." Since it was my job to clean the house, much of the hurtful lines my mother threw at me were related to my housecleaning abilities.

She'd inspect my work, sometimes with a white-glove test. She'd peer under the beds to see if I'd vacuumed. If I failed her "test" in any way, the litany began: "I don't know what's wrong with you. Nobody ever had to teach me how to clean a house. But you're a real dumb bunny." I always knew when the barrage was coming – fireworks shot off in my gut when my mother opened her mouth.

I dealt with this emotional pain on my own. I stopped defending myself when my mother yelled and looked at me in disgust. While silencing my voice kept me alive and relatively sane growing up, these coping mechanisms didn't help me as an adult. When I was in college this silence survival skill relegated me to the role of secretary and note taker during group projects. When I did speak up, I stumbled over my words. A well-meaning professor who noticed my lack of influence chided other students, telling them they never listened to me. While I felt supported, I was also deeply embarrassed by my ineffectual behavior. I was still responding to the constant recordings of parental voices in my head, telling me, "You're not good enough. You don't know what you're talking about. You're just a dumb bunny."

My lack of emotional intelligence skills continued to plague me when I entered the workplace, where I heard any type of feedback as criticism. Fresh out of graduate school at age 23, I took a job at Monsanto Co. in the internal audit department. We worked for different supervisors on each project, and when we closed out a project, we'd get a one-on-one review from that supervisor.

One Friday, when I had completed a four-week project, my 45-year-old supervisor said to me, "Look, you took too large of a sample size for the audit, so you wasted your time and overreached the project scope." I burst into tears. I still remember I was wearing a Kelly green dress, and how flummoxed my supervisor was by my emotional display. She had no idea what to do next.

That night, my primary supervisor called me at home. "Why did you have to cry in front of her?" he asked me. I gave him a rundown of the feedback, which I interpreted as criticism.

"OK, from now on I'm going to do your final reviews," my supervisor said. "You should have known I'd go to bat for you, but it's going to be more difficult now."

When we hung up, I felt even worse, of course. I spent the rest of the weekend beating myself up emotionally for my perceived work failure.

I realize that if I'd been skilled in emotional intelligence, I could have approached the whole crying-at-work scenario with a different, much more constructive attitude. Rather than defensiveness, I could have expressed curiosity. When the supervisor told me I'd used too large a sample size, I could have asked a question, "OK, what's your thought process on that? Why would you suggest a smaller sample size? What are you basing that on?"

I could have used the experience as a way to learn more about how to do my job well, plus presenting myself as an engaged and inquiring employee. Whether or not I agreed with the explanation, I might or might not have decided to voice my opinion. But my decision, either way, wouldn't have been based on a self-perception of inferiority and ineptitude.

It would be several years before I started delving deeply into emotional intelligence. I cried again, when I first took the EQ-i 2.0 assessment and read my results. They weren't what I hoped they'd be. I wondered how my results could be so low, since I'd engaged in years of therapy to work through my emotional issues. It was true I'd done a lot of work using a depth psychology approach. What I began to realize was that I also needed a more cognitive approach, and that both approaches combined could be a powerhouse. For example, I scored very high in empathy, but low in assertiveness. I needed to work to obtain balance in my emotional skillset. In fact, the Bar-On model emphasizes the need for balance among the various skills.

To summarize, what's become clear to me is to be effective in your life, especially in the workplace, you must integrate the realms of both logic and emotion. One of my mentors believes this is what can save the world. We've been told for years that IQ is king, and emotional intelligence is nothing more than a soft skill.

However, the research continues to show that IQ gets you in the door in the work world – after all, you need a level of technical proficiency in your field. But once you're in the door, to keep your job and to rise in the ranks, emotional skills are what's key.

I wrote this book to introduce you to this amazing skillset that can take you to heights of success and achievement you'd never achieve without them. You'll find it an exciting and a very rewarding journey. It's certainly been true for me!

How to Use This Book

When I counseled professionals at my private practice about navigating their personal and family relationships, I noticed they also talked to me about their work issues. The same emotional skills they needed to build at home to be fluid and happy in their home lives were the same exact ones they needed to be productive and happy at work, too.

In this book, I explore how taking emotions to work can enhance your professional life, and also be the make-or-break difference that takes you from being stuck in less-than-optimal performance to stellar success and professional brilliance. Using the conceptual model of emotional intelligence developed by Dr. Reuven Bar-On, I explore 16 fundamental emotional skills vital to your career success.

I've included journaling suggestions and exercises at the end of each chapter, as well. I encourage you to choose which exercises resonate with you, in addition to recording your insights as you read in a journal. Jotting down what happens during your day and how you felt, along with noting what you'd like to have done better or differently, will make a huge difference in your progress.

You might want to start by exploring your thoughts and feelings about emotion in the workplace in general. Does it have a place there? Or have you always viewed it as something that should be kept separate, reserved for a private sphere – your personal life only? How has emotion served as a positive factor in the workplace, and how has it, in your opinion, caused more trouble than it was worth, whether for you or a coworker?

Make a list of all the jobs you've had. Describe their various work environments and how they felt to you. Did you thrive? Or did you struggle? What were your work relationships like, both with your superiors and your direct reports? Were you happy and productive? Or did you count the hours till the day was finished and you could escape? As you reflect, create a list of situations you recall as being challenging. Keep these situations in mind as you read through my client profiles, looking at how their choice to evolve their emotional intelligence played a significant role in their success.

To get us started, here the most common challenges my clients face in their professional lives, many of which you'll recognize in your own work life:

- Feeling anxious and pressured about staying organized

- Not knowing how to prioritize their task list and stay on track

- Avoiding or procrastinating on certain job responsibilities or not fulfilling commitments

- Not taking control of frustrating and ineffective appointments or meetings

- Fearing personal or idea rejection from a boss or coworkers

- Lacking self-confidence in professional or networking situations

- Not making a conscious effort in their professional activities to work toward ultimate career goals

- Wasting time and energy on non-revenue-generating or career-advancement activities

- Generating insufficient revenue to pay bills and save for retirement

- Lacking a work-life balance, especially during the holidays or summer

- Inconsistently tracking productivity measures, such as sales activities, including how many calls they made, how many qualified prospects they're working with, how many appointments they made or kept, number of portfolio analyses they've performed, and so on, if they're in a financial role

- Failing to ask clients for referrals to grow their business, if they're in a financial or sales role

- Avoiding cold-calling prospects or struggling to effectively respond to objections and close deals, if they're in a sales position.

I believe, and research has proven, the amount of money you earn is
directly correlated to how high your emotional intelligence quotient is,
so business owners and professionals who master the 16 essential emotional intelligence skills I teach in this book will improve their profitability and success from day one.

The Bar-On EQ-I 2.0 Model of Emotional Intelligence: Five Composites and 16 Skills

In this section, you'll learn more about Dr. Reuven Bar-On's Model of Emotional Intelligence that I employ when exploring and improving emotional intelligence skills with business owners and their staff.

After years of study and research, Dr. Bar-On identified specific, measurable competencies from his initial broad definition of emotional and social intelligence: These 16 core skills are grouped into five composites, which you'll learn about in the following case study chapters.

First, let me tell you how my process generally works. When a business owner asks me to work with her and select employees to improve their workplace collaboration and culture, I start with the EQ-i 2.0 assessment tool: Dr. Bar-On created the Bar-On Emotional Quotient Inventory (EQ-i 2.0) to measure these skills. It's built on his proven system that effective emotional and social functioning leads to your overall sense of psychological well-being.

I use the EQ-i 2.0 leadership report if the person I'm assessing is a leader and manages people, and the workplace report if the person is an individual contributor who doesn't manage a team. The assessment results are a starting point for me to create a development plan to build and balance the 16 emotional intelligence skills. In addition, I run a Myers-Briggs personality assessment to round out the whole picture of each person. Then, I work with each team member to build and balance the 16 skills, effectively raising that person's emotional quotient – and their workplace success.

Clients have different goals based on their assessment results and their industry, but generally they all want to raise their emotional intelligence, or EQ. I have access to research data across different industries showing the top five EQ skills a person needs to become a Star Performer in their field, which I use to guide each client's development plan. (Did you know Star Performers outpace average performers by 127%? That's a good reason to raise your staff's EQ.)

For example, many business owners need to form stronger connections with their employees and clients, so we focus on empathy as one of their five key skills. Empathy is the ability to put yourself in your employee's or customer's shoes and relate to what they're feeling – and it can go a long way in building trust in these key relationships.

Without that trust, your employees and clients may think you're not listening, and they could walk away from your business. The more your employees feel listened to and understood, the more engaged and motivated they'll be while at work. Plus, since they're your brand ambassadors, your clients will love working with your firm, and will refer others to you.

Now let's take a step back. Before you feel empathy for others, you need to cultivate your own emotional self-awareness, an understanding of your feelings. That's because emotional self-awareness and empathy work together: By learning to understand, manage and control your emotions, you can use them to feel empathy for your employees and clients.

I'm sure you'll relate to this: You need to manage your emotional responses during a frustrating, charged meeting with an employee or client. If you lose your cool, you create a rift with a staffer or customer, distancing them from you. While it's possible to recover ground you lost in a professional relationship, people sometimes choose to move on to other employers or partners.

So what does all this mean in practical terms for your personal and professional life? When you're emotionally intelligent, you understand and accept your strengths and weaknesses, and express your thoughts and feelings constructively. You successfully cope with the stress of your daily demands, challenges and pressures. Your general mindset is optimistic, positive and self-motivating.

On an interpersonal level, you understand and relate well to others because you're aware of and can understand their emotions, feelings and needs, and you can forge cooperative, constructive and mutually satisfying relationships.

Because life isn't static, when you're emotionally grown up, you're OK with managing the dynamic nature of personal, social and environmental change by coping with your current situation. You can solve personal and interpersonal problems head-on without procrastinating. Plus, since you live in integrity with yourself, you can understand and process accompanying emotions in a way that works for your needs, goals and aspirations.

Here are more detailed descriptions of Dr. Bar-On's 16 skills organized into five composites, which we'll delve into in this book, so you can learn to master them in your own life.

Self-Perception Composite

> Think of self-perception as the work of the "inner self." The skills in the Self-Perception Composite are designed to assess your feelings of inner strength and confidence. In addition, you should pursue relevant and meaningful personal goals, while understanding the what, when and how different emotions impact your thoughts and actions.

Self-regard is possessing a core of self-confidence and inner strength that allows you to respect yourself while non-judgmentally understanding your strengths and weaknesses. When you have a high level of self-regard, you're self-assured, have a good sense of self and feel fulfilled in your life. When you're struggling with self-regard, you're unsure of yourself, have low self-esteem, don't respect yourself and are often critical of your personal appearance.

In the workplace, a professional with high self-regard is seen as a leader who exerts her influence on key, strategic decisions; stands by her viewpoints even when faced with dissents; and leads by capitalizing on her strengths and delegating her tasks in weaker areas. A person with high self-regard should stay mindfully aware of her strengths and weaknesses, and be willing to admit mistakes and accept constructive feedback from team members.

An individual with low self-regard on the job isn't seen as a leader; often, this person simply fades into the background. He doesn't share ideas and is often afraid to step outside of his comfort zone. Colleagues may call him a Dan Downer, as his low self-esteem causes him to put himself and others (and their ideas) down.

Self-actualization is your willingness to persistently try to improve yourself, pursuing relevant and meaningful activities that lead you to a rich and enjoyable life. This skill is strongly linked to your overall work success and performance; it can be summed up as: "pursuit of meaning." As a leader, that means finding purpose (you feel you're "right where you're meant to be") and enjoyment in your role, and performing to your fullest potential, in addition to setting challenging goals for yourself and your team.

A professional with high self-actualization is passionate and inspired about her role at her company, and lives her life in accordance with her personal values. She's dedicated to consistently leveraging her talents, as well as her team's, which means she's the locus of exceptional individual and team performance. This leader excels in creating a productive corporate culture where employees have a strong sense of morale and fulfillment so they can accomplish great feats in their careers.

On the other hand, some professionals with very high self-actualization may have unrealistic expectations of what their staff can actually accomplish. Plus, these staffers may not share the same level of enthusiasm for their work and corporate goals, so in this case, leaders should use their reality testing and empathy to gauge team engagement to motivate everyone.

Emotional self-awareness is the ability to accurately recognize and understand your feelings. You can differentiate subtleties in your own emotions while understanding their cause and the impact they have on your (and others') thoughts and actions. As a leader, if you have a clear understanding of how you generate emotions, it's easier for you to regulate your behavior and control the impact your emotions have on your employees.

Emotionally self-aware professionals lead and communicate with composure, generating admiration and respect from coworkers and employees. Since they have a thorough grasp of their emotional triggers and reactions, they can effectively navigate workplace challenges and difficult situations. They take time to contemplate their (and others') emotional responses instead of impulsively reacting. Because they grasp subtle emotional nuances, they can take calculated risks to help their organization meet its strategic goals.

However, professionals who need to work on their emotional self-awareness often lose their composure during tense work situations and say and do rash things that negatively affect others. In addition, those who are very self-aware may rely on their "gut feelings" and intuition too much when making decisions. It's important to seek opinions from colleagues and team members so you can support your proposed course of action.

Self-Expression Composite

> This composite is an extension of the Self-Perception Com-
> posite, and addresses the outward expression or action re-
> sulting from a person's internal perception. Within this
> skillset, you assess your ability to remain self-directed and
> openly expressive of your thoughts and feelings, while com-
> municating these feelings in a constructive and socially ac-
> ceptable way.

Emotional expression is the ability to effectively express your feelings verbally and non-verbally in a way that's genuine and consistent,
and isn't hurtful to others. Coworkers and employees are comfortable
around you because they usually know where you stand, and you find
beneficial ways to express your emotions, positive (i.e., appreciation) and
negative (i.e., frustration).

Leaders with strong emotional expression drive a culture of open
communication, so their team and others in the organization feel comfortable sharing ideas and concerns. In addition, these types of leaders
make decisions harmoniously, resolving interpersonal conflict and scoring resources. Emotionally expressive leaders inspire high levels of engagement in their team because they express passion for their work and
connect on a "feeling" level with employees.

Professionals who are too emotionally expressive, though, may overwhelm a team into being withdrawn, In addition when you over-share
emotion, others may perceive that you're ruled by your feelings, say,
if you continue to appear angry over a lost sale even after your team
has moved forward. It's better to consistently practice active listening
and mutual respect. That way, when your coworkers or employees feel
heard and understood, they're less likely to be defensive when you offer a differing point of view. Emotions backed by logic work best; for
example, "If we don't test the product thoroughly, I'm concerned we'll
lose thousands with a late or defective product."

Independence means you can think, feel and work on your own,
and be free of emotional dependency. In leadership, this is a critical
skill, since you can form your own ideas and then make decisions for
the team's greater good, without being swayed by popular opinion.

Independent leaders can analyze a situation, formulate a response
and start executing without second-guessing: This is critical because
leaders must be able to make difficult decisions quickly with limited di-

rection. However, they're able to seek input from their teams and take those opinions into account. Independent professionals aren't shy about adding their perspectives to discussions to influence their organization's strategic decisions.

Leaders who are too independent may not receive enough buy-in from their team if they act too autonomously. They may be viewed as a know-it-all, a leader who ignores facts or one with a closed-door policy, distancing them from their team. It's a good idea to seek input from key team members and then consider that feedback before presenting a counter-thought or making a final decision.

Assertiveness is your ability to express your feelings, beliefs and thoughts in a clear and confident way, and defend your rights in a non-destructive manner. Assertive leaders find the right language at the right time to express their feelings and thoughts. They're firm and direct when making decisions. They guide their teams toward their goals by articulating their needs and protecting their resources. They protect both their personal and team's rights.

Assertive leaders use this skill to gain their team's buy-in and lead them toward innovative solutions; it also helps them gain the resources their team needs to overcome obstacles and achieve goals. They're able to make decisions easily and resolve conflict. They're also not afraid to showcase their talents and their team's accomplishments companywide.

Leaders should take care that their behavior doesn't cross the line into aggression by failing to listen to others' input when they make decisions. In addition, some situations will require more flexibility, so a leader who becomes too rigid or stubborn in defending his position might miss information that could alter his perspective.

Interpersonal Composite

> The skills in the Interpersonal Composite focus on developing and maintaining relationships based on trust and compassion. You learn how to sensitively articulate an understanding of another person's perspective. It's also important to take care of your own needs, while still showing real concern for others, your team at work, or your greater community or organization.

Interpersonal relationships skills are when you can establish and maintain mutually satisfying relationships characterized by intimacy, and by giving and receiving affection. Good leaders use people and relationships to get the job done by gaining buy-in and commitment, and obtaining the resources their team needs to get the job done. These professionals usually try to understand each team member individually, while knowing their team's strengths and weaknesses. They also build out useful organizational relationships beyond their team, and then share those benefits with their staffers.

Leaders who value maintaining confidences, team harmony and open communication in their personal relationships bring that view into the workplace: These qualities automatically endear them to their employees and help build loyal relationships. By maintaining this rapport, these leaders motivate employees toward challenging and innovative goals.

While building interpersonal relationships with their teams, leaders should remember to recognize staffers' efforts on a regular basis and coach by delivering constructive feedback, to help their team reach individual and group potential. It's also key to remember what types of recognition motivates each staffer (not everyone likes "Happy Birthday" sung at their desk).

Empathy is the ability to recognize, understand and appreciate the way others feel – it's a crucial component in building strong interpersonal relationships. Empathetic leaders are viewed as approachable and authentic because their team feels safe sharing thoughts and ideas, and they care about their team's thoughts and feelings as much as they care about their own. Empathetic leaders satisfy their employees' human desires to feel heard and understood, leading to positive conflict resolution and gaining commitment to achieve goals.

Sometimes under stress, leaders can take a less empathetic approach, for example, not considering their team's needs when making a decision. On the flip side, stressed or upset leaders can let their empathetic side go, causing an emotional disconnect between them and their team, resulting in future trust issues.

Social responsibility in leadership means that you act in a morally responsible way, promote the greater good and be a strong voice for your team, company and community. These leaders demonstrate a social conscience and coach those they lead. They often act as a Good Samaritan who doesn't want anything in return for their help. They gain fulfillment from many sources, including activities outside work. Socially responsible leaders believe in building morale, mentoring and other development practices that build talent in their teams and organizations.

On the flip side, while leaders should support others, they should be aware of taking on too many responsibilities to the detriment of their own work, emotional state, goals or well-being. In addition, leaders also have to let their employees become independent and grow on their own.

Decision-Making Composite

The Decision-Making Composite skills focus on the way a person uses emotional information to make decisions, including the ability to resist or delay impulses as well as remain objective to avoid rash behaviors and ineffective problem solving.

Problem solving is what leaders do every day – but in emotional intelligence, they need to recognize how emotions affect their decisiveness. For example, they can work through the many steps to solving a problem without being emotionally distracted; they can also delve into touchy problems, understanding the emotions involved.

Skilled problem solvers display focus and a rational demeanor as they brainstorm solutions. They can reframe problems in a new way, helping their teams creatively generate solutions. In addition, they're often called on to solve problems because they can view a problem from different perspectives, without letting emotion take over.

Though appearing calm and collected, leaders also need to demonstrate to their teams that they're emotionally invested in the decisions they're making on behalf of their employees. That includes asking team members for opinions and feedback when reviewing potential solutions to problems.

Reality testing is a key component of how leaders make decisions: whether your approach is grounded, objective, and in touch with the reality of your work environment, or disconnected and biased. Good leaders try to stay objective as they tune in to what's happening around them, and provide clear, realistic direction based on information and facts to their team. In addition, they can view each person and situation as unique, while also having clear and consistent ethical views. Their coaching and performance management discussions are also free of personal bias and grounded in documented information and events.

Leaders should remember that emotions are there to provide information about an event, so ignoring them completely can mean they're missing out on data that that an objective analysis can't provide. Doing gut checks and tuning in to emotional information in their relationships can help keep them grounded. Finally, keeping up-to-date data available to fuel strong decisions is key, along with making that information available to staffers and encouraging them to use it to make well-informed decisions.

Impulse control is the ability to think before acting and to show restraint in the face of impulses and temptations to act. Leaders with high impulse control are viewed as highly stable, composed and methodical in their approach since they steer clear of rash conclusions and impatient behavior, incorporating appropriate analysis into every move. These leaders' focus and deliberate planning achieve corporate buy-in and trust. Under difficult circumstances, they're still able to stay composed and don't make knee-jerk decisions.

Sometimes, leaders with a lot of impulse control are seen as predictable and calculated, so be sure to be flexible enough to pay attention to your instincts or take part in spontaneous conversations. In addition if you work in a culture where action is valued more than contemplation, your team may think you can't drive change; to "unfreeze," decide what information you have to make a decision so you can devote the right amount of time to making a well-thought-out, but speedier decision.

Finally, employees respect leaders who can admit their mistakes and offer an apology.

Stress Management Composite

> In the Stress Management Composite, we look at how well we can cope with the emotions sparked by change, as well as unfamiliar and unpredictable circumstances, while remaining hopeful about the future and resilient in the face of setbacks and obstacles.

Stress tolerance is the ability to withstand adverse events and stressful situations without "falling apart" by actively and positively coping with stress. Strong leaders withstand intense pressures with a stoic calm and agilely cope with downsizing or competitive threats, for example. Their teams view them as taking decisive, prompt action when faced with complex issues or stressful events. This, in turn, motivates their teams to cope with uncontrollable events.

Leaders should remember that not everyone copes as well with pressure, so they should install safety nets like flexible work hours and stress management workshops in times of crisis. During regular work times, it's important to remember too that not all employees can handle the same volume of work, so communicating clear expectations and maintaining an open-door policy is key.

Finally leaders should assess their stress tolerance for certain projects, ensuring that they realistically can balance simultaneous projects with their current team members and resources.

Flexibility requires leaders to adjust their emotions, thoughts and behavior to changing situations and conditions in the office. Flexible leaders are comfortable with minor and major transformations, and are quick to respond to unpredictable events. They're reactive, and not stuck in traditional and outdated methods, ensuring that their team operates in a culture where new insights and perspectives are welcomed.

Leaders should make decisions armed with sufficient information to make a sound course of action, in addition to paying attention to their instincts and reality testing. Remember that employees want leaders who remain true to their beliefs and don't appear wishy-washy or too heavily swayed by others' opinions.

Optimism, the ability to look at life's brighter side and to maintain a positive attitude, even in the face of adversity, separates successful leaders from the rest of the pack. When these leaders face adversity, they overcome the challenge, learn from it and inspire others to do the same as they in turn tackle problems.

In meetings, leaders should monitor their speech to see if they're creating a positive or negative space. Using phrases such as "That sounds promising" and "Did you consider the alternative," can boost your positive mindset. Another tactic is to focus on your strengths and delegate tasks you don't excel at to a colleague. You'll leverage your skills to the fullest, and again aid in fostering a positive outlook.

The Well-Being Indicator

Happiness is the ability to feel satisfied with your life, to enjoy yourself and others, and to have fun in the present. It's different from the other emotional intelligence skills because it both contributes to and is a product of emotional intelligence. Your happiness level is an indicator of your emotional health and well-being.

The four subscales most associated with happiness are self-regard, self-actualization, interpersonal relationships and optimism. Since happiness is so connected with all emotional intelligence skills, though, leaders can discover further development opportunities if they explore how the remaining subscales contribute to their happiness level, and vice versa.

Part I

Self-Perception Composite

Story One: Maria

self-regard: the ability to respect and accept yourself as basically good.

You're in a meeting with your boss and other team members to brainstorm ways to market your company's newest product, an energy drink for athletes. You prepped for the speedy idea-generation session by jotting down five unique ways to get the word out to prospects and clients. You're proud of your ideas, especially the one about hosting an Instagram contest where customers post snaps of themselves in a unique location sipping the drink during their workout.

Yet, the meeting doesn't go the way you hoped. As your boss goes around the table asking each team member for ideas, you lose confidence in yours as you listen to everyone else. "Wow," you think, "my ideas just aren't as great as Grace's, Jim's and Jamie's. I better not say anything at all."

When your boss finally gets to you, you say, "Oh, everyone covered my ideas already. I don't have anything to add." Your boss looks at you, disappointed, as you crumple up your notes.

Has something like this ever happened to you in a work meeting? It probably has, to some degree.

This self-doubt is directly related to self-regard, EQ-i 2.0's foundational skill. Think of it as self-confidence, being at home with yourself and feeling worthy. It's standing up for yourself and speaking your mind, even if your ideas aren't popular and no one's listening. The key to self-regard is developing the ability to respect and accept yourself as basically good, and trusting yourself to make good decisions.

The three skills – self-regard, self-actualization and emotional self-awareness – comprising the Self-Perception Composite are crucial, because as my mentor and coach Dana Ackley stresses, you must possess enough self-regard to work on the other skills. You need a critical amount of ego strength – that's resiliency, fortitude, courage and non-defensiveness – to change thoughts and emotions that don't support your whole, greater self's goals and visions. In my practice, if a client's self-regard is low, our initial work focuses on developing this skill to support mastering the others.

Remember the story about my early career days at Monsanto when I cried at one of my performance reviews? My ego strength was fragile then and I perceived any type of constructive feedback as criticism. Had my self-regard and reality testing (that's your ability to assess the interaction between what you're experiencing and what objectively exists) been higher back then, I would have realized my supervisor was offering constructive feedback for my benefit.

Young people whose parents neglected their emotional and spiritual needs as children demonstrate how important it is to develop self-regard by the time they're adults. In my practice, I've worked frequently with people who grew up feeling emotionally abandoned or rejected by parents who were too absorbed with their own problems to raise them whole-heartedly. In many cases, these young girls and boys learn to raise themselves.

Additionally, trauma, chaos or drama existed in the original family household, repeatedly exposing the children to an exaggerated threshold of what would be a normal expression of emotion. This sets up an adult pattern of seeking ever-increasing amounts of chaotic intensity, which they believe they need to feel alive and enervated. Without the manufactured chaos and drama, they're bored and disengaged.

The problem: They don't understand their drama threshold is far above normal, to the point of being self-destructive in many cases, and the chaos they compulsively seek negatively impacts their self-regard, draining them emotionally and physically. Quite often, men and women who grew up in these households unconsciously gravitate toward narcissistic partners. This is usually an attempt, through repetition compulsion, to repair the parental wound by creating a safe, secure attachment to a romantic partner. This doesn't work because narcissistic partners have difficulty achieving genuine emotional intimacy and a secure attachment.

By the time these men and women seek professional help, their self-regard can be seriously eroded, with consequences impacting every facet of their lives, including their career. Low self-regard often prevents them from achieving top-performer status. Here's why: Although they're talented, these adults aren't as assertive as their peers. They don't share ideas in business meetings since they fear and avoid criticism – their bosses, teams and peers then see them as unprofessional and weak.

Yet, that's not the case: They're resilient, strong survivors who need to gain clarity about what matters most to them, so they can find their voice and assert themselves. In my experience, when these people build self-regard, they become more comfortable with themselves and their outward-facing persona transforms. This was certainly the case with Maria.

Maria's Story

Maria was a sassy woman from Georgia with flaming red hair and green eyes. At 40, she had a curvy figure that came from spending her free time at the gym. She was an avid weightlifter and a very skilled kayaker.

However, Maria's job in a dental practice was in jeopardy because she was consumed with her personal problems while at work, and increasingly started coming in late or calling out.

Her manager, Trevor, loved that Maria was excellent with patients, due to her strong interpersonal relationship skills, her ability to establish and maintain mutually satisfying relationships characterized by intimacy and by giving and receiving affection. In particular, she displayed a great amount of empathy, because she was aware of, understood and appreciated others' feelings.

When anxious patients came in for root canals, Maria was particularly skilled at soothing them because she mindfully explained the process to them. Patients raved to Trevor about how helpful Maria was in answering all their questions without rushing.

However, when it came to paperwork, it was a different story. Although Maria could give a patient her full attention, she struggled to work independently while processing patient information, files and invoices. While at her desk alone, she daydreamed and worried about her personal problems instead of working conscientiously.

Maria's manager didn't want to let her go because she was skilled at working with difficult patients, so Trevor referred her to me. In my professional practice, I'm hired by business owners for executive coaching to help them with their own leadership skills, and to coach some of their select employees who I feel have hidden potential, which is thwarted by their inability to contain and manage their emotions.

The Evaluation

A number of factors held Maria back from valuing her talents and fully committing to her job. A chronic binge eater, Maria took college courses several different times, but hadn't completed a degree, preventing her from moving up in her chosen field. Her parents, who divorced when she was a teenager, hadn't affirmed her worth as a child, so Maria grew into a needy and emotionally dependent adult.

Since Maria didn't view herself as worthy, she often developed feelings for emotionally manipulative or unreliable men who paid attention to her, appearing to accept her. Once involved in chaotic and unhappy relationships, Maria didn't say "no" or erect boundaries to protect her own self-regard. Not surprisingly, the toxicity in Maria's relationships drained her energy, causing her to disengage at work – and also in our meetings – so my goal was to build a safe, steady and reliable relationship with her.

Maria's EQ-i 2.0 assessment revealed that she scored very low in the Self-Perception Composite; building self-regard in a person who scores low in this composite is a challenging process. I measure progress in small increments that take root and thrive, rather than in great leaps, which leave my client open to regression. With Maria, I initially cheerleaded and helped reinforce her sense of self, building the foundation crucial for her to master other emotional skills.

For example, after Maria missed a session early on, I contacted her, reiterating my intention to help her become happier at home and work. She admitted the reason it was difficult for her to stay connected to our work: If she made herself vulnerable and shared her story she feared I'd judge her.

We started to make progress, though. Maria felt misunderstood and blamed for her shortcomings at her job. In a non-judgmental way, I explained how her behavior affected her personal and professional life. This was a turning point in our work because Maria worked to stay engaged despite receiving constructive criticism. "One of the most important things I learned," Maria told me, "was that we can agree to disagree and still stay in a relationship." She trusted the reciprocal nature of our relationship, and viewed me as working on her behalf as much as I was working for her manager.

The Work

There are many tools and techniques to build your positive self-regard. Creative expression is an excellent way to develop this skill. For example, many people enjoy writing, regardless of which form it takes: journaling, fiction, nonfiction, prose or poetry. Maria employed a combination of journaling, writing poetry and dreamwork to grease the wheels of her emotional self-awareness and to alter her self-perception. Since I'm trained in Jungian dreamwork through the Haden Institute, I encourage clients to write down their dreams and we review the content for guidance on practical life matters.

When Maria started writing, she discovered she wanted illustrations to accompany her writing, so she took up sketching scenes that were meaningful to her life. The act of looking deeply at and interacting with the physical world gave Maria a sense of being grounded, which she had rarely experienced before.

Our next step was for Maria to use these newfound skills to stay productive at work, especially on days when she felt preoccupied with events in her personal life. I asked her to bring a journal to work: When she had a negative, distracting thought she wrote it in the journal, took three deep breaths to calm her central nervous system and closed the book.

This technique worked so well we added to it: Maria pasted a sketch of her pet in the notebook. While taking her deep breaths, she looked at the photo, helping her reconnect to positive feelings of love and support. Ultimately, she generated these feelings just by thinking about her pet at work. Similarly, because Maria loved nature, I suggested she keep flowers on her desk and also eat lunch outdoors beneath a tree. This gave Maria a refreshing pause in the middle of her workday, raising her energy levels to spend the afternoon on patient paperwork.

In tandem, we reviewed the situations Maria wrote down that triggered her unhappy or unpleasant emotions. I suggested practical examples of alternate behaviors so Maria could confidently handle her workload when she had these thoughts. We also discussed other ways to view stressful situations so she didn't immediately view them as insurmountable obstacles. Once this creative approach became easier for Maria, she learned to change her thoughts and emotions about herself, radically improving her level of self-regard.

This is a good place to discuss the importance of integrity as you're building your self-regard: Integrity is being honest with yourself, and staying true to your core principles you've defined for yourself. That core value changed my life when I first started practicing it and developing a relationship with myself: being true to my inner wise woman, hearing her message and honoring it in the form of action. I shared with Maria examples of how my first therapist helped me develop my personal sense of integrity.

For example, I regularly talked with Maria about her work week. "You know, when you have a fight with your boyfriend and you come in the office late or leave early because you're emotionally drained, who does that affect most?" I'd say.

"Well, I guess people in the office might think I'm acting flakey," Maria would muse and get upset.

"Let's look at this another way," I'd say. "Letting a fight with your boyfriend affect your job performance isn't a good use of your integrity. It affects you and your life. Think of it like that, rather than on how other people in your office might judge that behavior."

As we talked more that way, I removed the emphasis on how coworkers judged her behavior and more on how Maria viewed her own actions. Then, something clicked. Maria started to understand how to empower herself by caring more about how she felt about herself, rather than how she perceived others saw her.

Maria learned to turn inward and examine her own conscience and behaviors instead of looking outward for approval and affirmation. Gradually this process of turning inward for self-validation took hold in Maria's psyche so it sounded like her own positive, mental voice.

The Results

During our work together, Maria witnessed and borrowed my process toward self-regard, that of turning inward to hear my authentic voice. She learned to access and develop her own voice and by activating her inner guidance system, started redirecting her life onto a positive path. She was eventually able to identify her own list of values and wants, including short- and long-term goals. Most important, she developed the courage to take action toward her goals without getting stuck in inactivity and distraction.

Maria developed a plan to follow through on completing her higher education and identified other ways to develop her financial and emotional self-sufficiency so she felt more comfortable at her job. This enabled her to talk to her manager, Trevor, and successfully enumerate the reasons she deserved a raise. Lobbying for and receiving a raise significantly boosted Maria's self-regard, and she began to work harder and smarter at her job.

Maria also realized she needed to end relationships that didn't support her deep-seated values and goals. After she separated from her current boyfriend, she made significant progress by realizing that staying in a relationship with a person who didn't support her growing self-regard was detrimental to her. This helped her make a deeper commitment to herself. At work she had more energy and was more focused. As a result, Maria's company helped fund her college courses.

Armed with a higher level of self-regard, Maria accepted that although not everything about her future was certain, she could always count on herself and her new discernment skills to guide her to the next best step. Toward the end of our work together, Maria told me, "I have an increasing sense of freedom as I shake off old residue from my past that caused me to make inappropriate decisions." She realized she had freed herself to walk into her future on her own terms.

Building Your Self-Regard

Let's review. Self-regard is your ability to respect and accept yourself as basically good. If you're unable to do that, you can't convey respect and acceptance to others in your personal and professional life. This is often my starting point with my clients, since many people carry guilt and shame about past experiences in their lives, which prevents them from presenting themselves confidently to others. When we work to erase guilty feelings, we create a collection of habits that guide how you view yourself.

One way I encourage my clients to build their self-regard is by helping them acknowledge they've always done the best they could with the resources they had at the time. Reframing "mistakes" as valuable life lessons can help you move forward. You can also make a list of accomplishments you're proud of in your personal and business life. Celebrate that list and really feel good about what you've achieved. In addition, make the intentional effort to catch yourself doing something right instead of watching for missteps. I've advised my clients to keep a nightly journal where they focus on three things they were proud of that day – this journaling built up their confidence, and was one of the most helpful things they did to increase their self-regard.

Exercises for Exploration and Mastery: Self-Regard

Now it's your turn. Each of the following exercises will help you change the habits you've developed for thinking about yourself, and enable you to increase your level of self-regard. Remember, self-regard originates from:

- what you believe you're good at, such as leading a team, handling customers or writing marketing copy, and

- who you believe loves and likes you in your personal and professional relationships.

Critical to a positive and healthy self-regard is having a satisfactory relationship with yourself. Of course this sounds straightforward, but it takes time, patience and perseverance to forge this relationship.

Choose the exercises that resonate most with you, and complete them in your journal before you move to the next chapter.

Exercise 1

On a scale from 0 to 100, how much do you like yourself these days?

How much would you like to like yourself? What's your goal (from 0 to 100)?

Your Takeaway: Evaluating where your self-regard is as you start this program and setting a goal is a great beginning.

Exercise 2

Consider what you'll gain when you raise your self-regard: the benefits to you, your company, and your family and friends.

Benefits to myself:

Benefits to my company:

Benefits to my family and friends:

Your Takeaway: When you work to up-level your self-regard, you won't just benefit yourself: Your company, family and friends will also reap the rewards.

Exercise 3

What's standing in the way of you nudging your self-regard level up to the number you picked in the first exercise? Think about these barriers. For example, if your current self-regard is 40, but you'd like to raise that number to 80, what's standing in your way? Do you believe you have to change something about yourself before you hit 80, or is it simply changing the way you think about yourself?

Now, write down your self-talk about this exercise. What does your inner voice say about you? Are these comments rational and fair? Would you talk to your spouse or good friend in the same way you're talking to yourself? If not, why not?

Your Takeaway: Consider being as kind to yourself as you might be to a friend, especially in the early stages of your journey.

Exercise 4

Write down your strengths, such as empathy, sense of humor, hard work and reliability. You can review your EQ-i 2.0 report for ideas as well.

Review this list daily, and add items to it. You'll think of more items the longer you practice this exercise, because you're changing your focus from the negative to the positive. It's a new way of viewing yourself. Now, write down at least one event a day that shows off your strengths. For example, "Today, I helped George close a sale," or "Today, I treated my team to a pizza party to reward them for a great first quarter."

Your Takeaway: Write your strengths on index cards, one strength or affirmative statement per card. Stand in front of a mirror. Read each strength out loud while you look into your own eyes. While you might feel awkward doing this at first, it'll work! This exercise programs your unconscious mind for success. You can use these cards before an important business meeting, conversation or sales call.

Exercise 5

Plan to talk with the people closest to you, at work and in your personal life. Ask them: What are my strengths? Add those qualities to your list of strengths in Exercise 4. Don't write down any criticisms. Now, list the people you'll chat with, and add their comments about you in when you speak to them.

Your Takeaway: Remember, other people see you differently than you see yourself. You'll be surprised by how positive these conversations are.

Story Two: Dustin

self-actualization: the ability to realize your potential capacities.
emotional self-awareness: the ability to accurately recognize your feelings.

Self-actualization saved my career, enabling me to try new things and take continuous steps to find my true passion. My father, who was the CFO of a large, well-known and family-owned office supply company, helped me develop this skill at an early age as I watched him tend his garden and constantly beautify and improve the woods surrounding our home.

At night and on the weekends, weather permitting, my father hard- and soft-scaped as if he were really a landscape architect. "It's important to have balance in your life," he told me. "If you're going to work hard in an office all week, you need to do something different to rejuvenate in your free time."

I noticed how passionate my father was about "working in the yard," as he called it, which he did for years for as long as he was physically able. He creatively looked at what was already beautiful and magnificent, conjuring up ways to make it better. In this way, he inspired my drive to constantly improve myself, and my quest to find more and more meaning and purpose in my life.

I saw him experiment and take risks: One year he planted apple and peach trees, along with strawberry and blueberry plants. Later he lamented the birds ate all the ripened fruit before we could harvest it for ourselves. The next season he used netting to protect the bushes and trees, outsmarting the birds.

Another time, I helped him build a storage shed to store his tractor from a kit. The tractor didn't fit in the shed after we finished: He had neglected to take proper measurements beforehand. Nonplussed, my father improvised by storing the tractor in the garage and moving garage items to the new shed. He viewed life as a series of experiments, constantly fine-tuning until he worked everything out.

When I earned my first undergraduate degree, I pursued accounting because my father was a CPA. I thought if I became a CPA, I'd be happy like he was. When I graduated with my bachelor of business administration degree in finance, I didn't know what type of a job I actually wanted to do, so I entered graduate school immediately. I studied multiculturalism, languages (I became fluent in French), accounting and finance, and that's how I scored the job in Monsanto's internal audit department.

People from my graduate school were attractive hires to Monsanto, which had plants and holdings all over the globe. At that point in my life, I didn't have the emotional self-awareness to understand I didn't get meaning and purpose from being an accountant. So, I continued to take more classes and study, earning my CPA as well as a master's degree in taxation. Whenever I wasn't feeling successful or happy, I thought the answer was getting more training, which is how I wound up with three graduate degrees.

Over time, I branched into public accounting and then asset-based lending. Every experience I had taught me something important, and the lessons I learned help me in my current career. It wasn't until I spent time in contemplation and reflection, especially during a True Work workshop with Justine and Michael Toms, co-authors of *True Work: Doing What You Love and Loving What You Do*. That's when I realized what my next, best step should be.

In the workshop, we contemplated identifying what we'd love to do, all day long, whether we got paid for it or not. That was how I reached the self-awareness to realize I read psychology books for fun, as if they were fiction books. I loved listening to people and friends about their longings in life, and I got fulfillment from helping them. That knowledge propelled me to earn another degree, and a license in marriage and family therapy, and I found fulfillment in opening my own business.

It was that same emotional self-awareness that called to me years later, to get certified as an Emotional Intelligence and Leadership Coach, which is why I'm speaking to you now. Having the emotional self-awareness to understand and correctly label your own emotions, needs and desires works with your self-actualization skills to call your soul and propel you forward.

In this chapter, we'll focus on two skills that round out the Self-Perception Composite: self-actualization and emotional self-awareness.

You may be aware that passion and talent often overlap: Self-actualization is about engaging and developing these passions and talents. We all share a basic desire to express ourselves, and also to self-develop and improve. When you mix these drives with passion, you involve yourself in activities that have a personal meaning to your life and your specific skills. Self-actualization measures the strength of these drives – the stronger these drives, the bigger your achievements.

People who possess high levels of self-actualization are successful at home and at work, because development and pleasure in one area of their life spurs development and pleasure in the other area. Unfortunately though, for many reasons, life experiences affect our ability to self-develop. For example, some families of origin don't encourage college education or entrepreneurship, and children who grow up with those messages can find it hard as adults to excel even if their natural inclinations are to earn a master's degree or start their own financial services company. A self-limiting parent might say, "Oh, a college degree? Guess you think you're better than the rest of us now."

Working hand-in-hand with self-actualization is emotional self-awareness: That's when you're able to recognize your feelings, differentiate between them, know why you're feeling these emotions and recognize how they impact those around you. We know emotions manifest physically through our bodies, in our thoughts and in our impulses; you can learn how to name your feelings by paying attention to these three areas unique to you.

When Dustin first contacted me, his doctor had just diagnosed him with a stress-related illness. Dustin felt overwhelmed and anxious about his work responsibilities managing employees at a nonprofit that served his community.

"I just don't feel like I have a strong marriage or working relationships," he told me. "I can't count on my wife to get things done at home. I don't have time to fix the 17 mistakes that my staffers shouldn't have made every single day." He had just gotten tired of trying to change this pattern at home and at work, and was ready to give up.

Dustin actually began his studies infused with high self-actualization, which he learned by watching his parents, who were both physicians, excel in their field. Both taught at a well-known hospital and received honors and acknowledgements for their career achievements. In addition, his mother kept a very clean house, and always had meals prepped and served at the same time every day. Dustin had high aspirations that led him to earn a Ph.D. in social work. However, EQ-i 2.0 is a snapshot in time; it doesn't stay static. Over the years, his self-actualization dipped quite low. In addition, he lacked emotional self-awareness and didn't know how to apply what he had learned about helping and serving others to help himself and his family.

Dustin's Story

Dustin was a 35-year-old hotshot from Colorado who used to be a professional snowboarder. Muscle-bound and fit, he was 6'5" and 200 pounds as he towered over me. By contrast, his wife was petite and slender, and tended to be shy and quiet. She liked to needlepoint pillows in her spare time.

Dustin was reluctant to communicate honestly and courageously with his wife and employees. He was also this way with me at first. Though he politely and quickly answered my introductory in-depth questions, I wondered how well-thought-out his responses could be, simply because he didn't know how to talk about his past life experiences and how they affected his life today. That was a large part of his suffering.

Withdrawal from others and avoiding emotional issues was a pattern for Dustin. He also avoided answering certain questions in the homework I gave him. For example, I asked him to reflect on and write out how he developed his expectations about life and marriage, but he refused to complete that assignment. His reluctance kept him stuck in a withdrawal pattern, both at home and work.

At home, he spent a lot of time working and studying in a separate room, while the rest of his family gathered together in the living area to socialize, eat or watch television. At work, he failed to communicate important priorities, goals and tasks to his coworkers and employees, and then wondered why his assistant and team didn't carry them out.

Dustin isolated himself from the people he loved and relied on so much. At the same time, he earnestly yearned for connection with them. "I wish I could come home after work and look forward to spending time catching up with my family," he told me. "That's the person I'd really like to be."

However, the choices he made trapped him in a box of his own making: He wanted his family to be different that than were, but he wasn't willing to share those thoughts with them because he was such a reluctant communicator.

Paradoxically, I prescribed the symptom. "Dustin, because you feel confined, I want you to try doing things that will put more space in the relationship between you and your family," I told him. "Use your creativity to identify activities that will fill you up and help you feel nourished." He decided he'd attend outdoor concerts and start weightlifting. I encouraged him to keep identifying relaxing, creative activities he could regularly engage in help him feel in the flow of life again. In addition, I asked him to spend time in quiet contemplation to offset and balance his busy work life.

Dustin also said he was a romantic guy who didn't feel romantic toward his wife. "I just feel indifferent and living in a typecast role," he told me. "To live in the manner and style my family has functioned in for many years, I had to stop caring about what I wanted. But being a non-caring person isn't my natural temperament."

This was because Dustin grew up in a well-run household, and by contrast his, with six young children, was chaotic, like a "revolving door," he told me. Besides each of the children constantly needing to be taken to different sports and extracurricular activities, his wife didn't run a fine-tuned household: Dirty dishes piled up in the sink, the children stayed up late watching TV, forgetting to do their homework, and clothes and toys littered the floor.

"I thought about different solutions: make my wife change, divorce her, have an affair or endure it," he told me. "The first three options weren't viable, so I chose the fourth." He withdrew from his marriage and children, a habit pattern that caused him great stress because he didn't understand it was the cause of his own internal and unconscious conflict.

Dustin felt the world played a cruel joke on him because he was naturally such an optimistic guy. Now he felt like he was going through the five stages of grief (denial, anger, bargaining, depression, acceptance and hope). Dr. Elizabeth Kubler-Ross elaborates these five stages in her book, *On Death and Dying*, which describes meaningful conversations between doctors and patients when receiving personal bad news about their health. This includes the aftermath of processing this news and the mind games a person might play with themselves after they learn they're terminally ill.

In addition to death, these five stages have been extrapolated and used by many others in an effort to cope with different kinds of personal loss, including the death of a loved one, divorce, losing a job, or even surviving natural disasters.

Dustin's family still made overtures to include him in family functions. His young wife still tried to be intimate with him, but he turned her down, telling me he avoided being alone with her as much as possible. For homework, I suggested he ask his wife how she felt when he declined her invitations, but he wasn't ready for this scary step yet. We spent time on his personal issues, though, because I believed they were at the core of his general work ennui.

Dustin believed men were passionate, emotional beings. "That's why I feel demoralized after years of feeling numb at home," he said. He didn't know how to feel loving and kind toward his family, because he had emotionally detached from them.

"Feeling something is better than feeling nothing," I told him. During our first meetings, he resisted communicating with his family, so in response, I switched gears and asked him to summon courage and passion for his work. We looked at his company's mission and vision statements to see where we could find a roadmap for his meaning and purpose. "Let's use your creativity to brainstorm ways of feeling more vital and alive in your workplace," I said.

Over time, I asked Dustin if he liked himself. "I do, but I'm exhausted," he told me. "My daily life is the movie *Groundhog Day*, where a weatherman finds himself inexplicably living the same day over and over again." He wasn't a fear-based person, but he was afraid. "In the past, I always had an answer, but right now I don't and I don't know what will work to change things for me at home and at work," he said.

"What's your personal definition of passion?" I asked.

"It's a confidence or energy where there's a willingness to be open to good things happening," Dustin answered quickly. Yet, he felt no personal connection to this at all and was afraid he wouldn't be able to stay open to it.

The Evaluation

When I ran Dustin's EQ-i 2.0 leadership report, we got some answers. His next-to-lowest scores were in self-regard and self-actualization, the two foundational building blocks of emotional intelligence. We had to start building those up before tackling optimism, his lowest score.

Though Dustin described himself as an optimist, he was barely functional in this skill, and hadn't scored highly on the happiness and well-being indicator.

In the past I always had an answer, but now I've no idea what will work to get me out of this funk, Dustin told me.

Though I wanted to help him raise his optimism level for immediate relief, I knew this wasn't possible because we needed to raise his low self-regard and self-actualization scores first, which would take time. I redoubled my efforts, helping him focus on making more time for creative, fun activities like listening to his favorite music, going to see new movies and working out. This was difficult for Dustin though, because he felt powerless to change anything in his life.

A turning point was my suggestion to practice seeing himself as optimistic, pragmatic and solutions-oriented. "You know, I used to see myself this way a long time ago," he told me.

"Of course, and you have a template in your brain from having higher self-regard at one point," I said reassuringly. "If you viewed yourself that way once, you can see yourself that way again."

We worked on his language to move him further down this path. "Let's consider the difference in feeling and tone between saying, 'I could have done something different' and 'I should have done something different,'" I said.

"'I could have' sounds better," Dustin said, and I agreed.

"This is our preferred way of speaking because it conveys you have a choice in your life, rather than reacting as a victim," I explained.

Dustin applied this new language to the way he talked about what was happening in his life with good results. I suggested adding in some mindfulness-based techniques, such as opening his heart and being more receptive to hearing answers to his own questions or focusing on doing the next right thing today instead of looking too far down the road and wondering what direction to take in the months ahead.

The Work

I asked Dustin to write down what he wanted the next 10 years of his life to look like because he had lamented, "I know how fast the next decade can go by, and I don't want to waste those years." I wanted him to make more intentional choices today that would be more aligned with his long-term life vision. However, during our next meeting after doing this exercise, Dustin said, "I'm not feeling any traction at all."

"What would traction look like for you?" I asked.

"Honestly, it's doing the next right thing," Dustin said. "I can't move forward because I feel so discouraged."

This was a conundrum for me because Dustin scored high in independence, the ability to work in a self-directed way without the constant need for reassurance from others. However, he scored lower in assertiveness, so I hypothesized that was where his reluctance to take charge or to generate a sense of agency originated.

Dustin believed how his family treated him was key to his happiness. He felt left out of the family dynamic because his children usually went to his wife for answers to their problems, or to ask permission to stay at a friend's house. "My wife doesn't direct them to me," said Dustin, who wanted to be seen as the head of the household. "She takes care of our children's needs and makes decisions about their activities."

When we dug deeper, I learned Dustin's children didn't want to go to him because he acted inflexible, usually saying "no" or offering little empathy for their plights. Acting as head of the household might sound attractive, but I recommended that ideally Dustin and his wife would work together as a team to raise their children, and wouldn't allow the children's behavior to drive a wedge between them.

"A large part of healthy assertiveness is the ability to initiate or take action," I told Dustin.

As we talked about these abilities, Dustin said, "I just feel lost and don't know what actions to take." For Dustin, feeling lost and powerless over his future was a common theme in his struggle.

Although Dustin lacked clarity, he was hungry for strategy, so that was a good sign. After completing self-reflection exercises, he said, "I want to feel confidence, joy, peace, happiness and contentment, but actually feel the complete opposite emotions: deflated, subdued and flat."

"Try using meditation as a way to de-stress and unplug from what you experienced as a feeling of chaos or constantly being on edge," I told him. "When you look at your situation, what can you learn from it? You'll see results if you do this."

The day finally came when Dustin realized he might be a victim of his own thinking. When he had this insight, his mindset was just beginning to shift, and he developed more consciousness about his work, wife and family. To reinforce these budding realizations, I suggested he read some books, including *The Hero's Journey* by Joseph Campbell and *Getting the Love You Want* by Harville Hendrix.

"Stop blaming other people for the source of your unhappiness," I told Dustin. "Look inside yourself and examine your part in the family system." He needed to identify the steps he could take to regain his optimism and make positive changes – without relying on other people. "Take some risks and give yourself credit for trying something different," I said.

A major turning point for Dustin was when he realized his wife and family wouldn't intentionally try to hurt him, and this helped soften his approach with them. "I'm recognizing I have to look at stuff in my life that hurts me and face that first to change my behavior," he said. "Until this point, I haven't really thought about the life experiences that bruised me and how they might have negatively shaped my thinking."

Since Dustin complained he had no photos of his wife, I told him to take one with his phone so he could carry it with him all the time. "Look at her picture often so that you can rebuild an intuitive connection with her," I suggested.

Then he worked on a self-evaluation for us to review. "Wow, I really see that what I'm feeling isn't good and I've developed a negative attitude," he said. "I'm sometimes aggressive, impulsive and dogmatic to a fault." Together, we developed a plan for him to change his attitudes and learn to hold himself accountable to new and positive thinking. Since he was unsure of himself, we focused on helping him build trust in what he was experiencing through his intuition.

As part of this plan, Dustin told me he realized he needed to retrain his mind to not be distracted from his sense of purpose. "Having a lack of order, or systematic way of doing things, held me back from achieving my goals," he said. "It's going to take a whole month of focusing on nothing but this one factor to succeed in reorganizing my life." I helped him find a phone app that helped him track and better manage his time, using it to develop what he referred to as a "consistency mindset."

Some of the most important information surfaced when we worked on building Dustin's self-regard. Remember, if a client's self-regard is low, we work on that skill first because it's foundational to all the other emotional intelligence skills.

"I'd really like to be better at setting and achieving goals, being more productive, living life in a more fulfilling way, becoming more focused and having a deeper vision, developing my creativity and increasing my problem-solving skills," said Dustin, who also realized he wanted to be more engaged with his family. "By withdrawing from them, I'm avoiding and escaping real intimacy," he said.

"So what you want to do is support and encourage each of your family members to accomplish their goals since that will make you feel happy," I said.

"Yes, and I also want to learn to care and still be vulnerable at the same time," he countered, and I explained this would require him to get to know himself better and give himself permission to step fully into the person he was at his core.

"Dr. Moore, the most important lesson I've learned through this process is I can't be good to anyone else unless I'm good to myself first," Dustin said.

The Results

Since Dustin was fearful of being disappointed by a lack of accomplishment, at first he was cautious about making his necessary changes. One of the reframed thoughts that helped him most was when we decided he could strive for change without any predetermined expectations of how things would turn out.

"I know it's difficult for you to stay in this mindset and you struggle to continuously adopt it, and this seems to be one of the missing ingredients to propelling you forward," I told Dustin. I reinforced this idea by asking him this prodding question: "Is there something you can do or steps you can take whether you produce results or not?"

As Dustin considered the answer to this question, he loosened up, and it gave him the space to try new behaviors, while relaxing his expectations of himself. "Think of the metaphor of loosening up constricting clothing, or loosening a tie that's too tight, and the feeling of physical relief accompanying that," I'd say to Dustin. That's the effect this question had on him.

From this point forward, we talked about how Dustin could be more intentional at work and at home. We developed an affirmation he used daily to focus his attention: "I desire to be fruitful, productive and efficient at work and at home."

Dustin started communicating more with his family and staff. "I want to redirect my vision and inspire my employees," he told me, so we focused on further developing his leadership skills. Since he wasn't in a position to hire additional staffers, he had to figure out how to best use available resources to accomplish his new strategic objectives.

"My employees are all hard workers, and I'm concerned that they're worn out because they look tired throughout the work day and drowsy in meetings," Dustin said. To find the answers to rejuvenating his team, Dustin spent a lot of time reflecting and planning: journaling, writing and figuring out ways to be a lot more organized. "I'm realizing that my ability to communicate with my staff directly affects their productivity and efficiency," he said.

"As the leader, you're the visionary," I told him. "The best way to inspire and engage your team is to truly be yourself." Over time, Dustin was amazed to see how his more positive attitude combined with increased communication made a major difference in the quality of his life.

At home, he noticed he and his wife related better and started to function as a team again, especially with situations concerning their children. They established daily routines so his personal life felt less hectic and more congruent. At work, Dustin was more responsible and accountable to himself and others. In fact, his office conducted a customer-satisfaction survey and learned the firm had a 97% approval rating among its clients.

"I'm so encouraged I'm making good progress," Dustin said. "One of the accomplishments I'm most proud of is how I've developed the ability to see the greater good in a situation instead of focusing on the negatives."

Building Your Self-Actualization and Emotional Self-Awareness

Self-actualization is the state of "constantly becoming" yourself. I think of it as a continual state of giving birth to your real, true self: You're searching for and following through with activities and pursuits that give you the most energy, or the most meaning and purpose in your life.

It's different than seeking perfection, which implies you're finished or complete, while self-actualization is a process that doesn't end. The goal of perfection is to be as flawless, or free from flaws, as you can possibly be. The goal of self-actualization has nothing to do with eradicating your flaws, and everything to do with discovering what motivates you and brings you success and fulfillment.

To have good self-actualization, you need to understand your emotions and where they're coming from – that's called emotional self-awareness. We can better understand our emotions by paying attention to our physical and bodily sensations, and our thoughts and our behaviors. All three of these indicators provide clues as to what the underlying emotions are in our daily reactions to people, events and situations. In addition, the more you understand yourself and your own emotions, the better you can understand someone else and their emotions.

Exercises for Self-Exploration and Mastery: Self-Actualization and Emotional Self-Awareness

One way I encourage my clients to improve emotional self-awareness is to "go meta" and observe their behavior as if they were watching themselves in a movie. I ask them to watch themselves on the imaginary screen and attempt to identify whether their body language and tone of voice is congruent with their supposed feelings. If they imagine a freeze frame at a significant juncture, can they label what they were really feeling – internally and then in response to an event, situation or person in the imagined movie?

Choose from more exercises below that resonate most with you, and complete them before you move to the next chapter.

Exercise 1

Start with the end of your life. If you had to write your obituary now, long before you actually die, can you project yourself into your future and imagine what you'd want it to say? Make a list of all the accomplishments you want to achieve. Also outline goals in these different aspects of your life: family, friends, self, career, education, spirituality, health and fun. Be as specific as you can. Write down your accomplishments as if they already happened. When you're finished, view this as your strategic plan. You can use it to work backward, and set goals for decades, years, months, days and even hours, all the way back to your present.

Your Takeaway: By doing this exercise, you're fast-forwarding your life five, 10 or 20 years from now, with the advantage of seeing what you ideally want to be doing. Study what you've written. What skills will you need to develop? What classes or trainings might you need to take? What degrees would you need to earn? This exercise is a true gift to create a roadmap for your ideal life.

Exercise 2

It's time to find your passion. Consider these questions: What would you do whether you got paid for it or not, just because you love doing it? How do you spend your free time? What do you enjoy reading about or studying? Can you figure out a pattern? If so, this can give you clues to what really motivates you.

Your Takeaway: You might learn something new about yourself – that you could turn one of your hobbies into a career.

Exercise 3

Write your mini-autobiography as a short journal exercise. Look for recurring themes and patterns. What kind of events excited you? What do you like, and not like, about your life and pursuits? What are you good at? What do other people say you're good at? What moments of your life were your greatest teachable moments, and what did you learn from them? If you could rewrite this narrative knowing what you know now, how would you rewrite it?

Your Takeaway: Reviewing your past and non-judgmentally considering what you've learned and what you might have done differently can help you chart a different course for your future.

Exercise 4

In what types of situations do you usually have trouble handling your emotions? For example, when a client cancels without sufficient notice, or worse yet, misses an appointment without a good reason, I can get triggered. Why? Because I usually spend time preparing for each client meeting, and when the appointment hour rolls around, I'm mentally and strategically ready. If there's been an accident on the highway, or someone's sick, of course I understand. However, if my client just doesn't feel like talking to me today, or she just wants to do something else, it's harder for me to understand. I have to stop to think and mentally prepare myself before I respond when this happens; otherwise I run the risk of my client thinking I don't care about her. Rehearsing this scenario in my mind over and over again, long before it happens, helps me prepare for the day it does happen. What about you?

Your Takeaway: Understanding and prepping for your triggering situations put you right in the driver's seat, enabling you to feel in control when these events occur.

Exercise 5

Learn to check out your emotions. Do you have a trusted advisor, friend or coach, someone you can turn to for help with processing your emotions? If you know and understand your triggers, then you know sometimes your emotional triggers can hijack your behavior and cloud your judgement. Running through a sticky or emotionally triggered situation by talking to this person about it can help you see and understand where your judgement is being clouded by your emotions.

Your Takeaway: Turning to a trusted person in your life for a non-judgmental view of your actions during a tough situation can help you make deliberate behavioral changes for the future.

Exercise 6

Stabilize your emotions. Here's something I learned from Dr. Keith Parker that's made a major difference to me. The trick with emotions is to not get too high (excited) or too low (depressed) in reaction to various life events. One of the problems I had when I was younger was regulating my emotions, which felt like going on an emotional roller-coaster ride. It's possible to govern your emotions so you feel them instead of them feeling you. Can you list events or situations you know are most likely to get you too excited or too depressed?

Your Takeaway: Imagine neutralizing your emotions, in response to these events you've listed, so you're not too high or too low.

Part II

Self-Expression Composite

Story One: Stacy

emotional expression: the ability to openly express your feelings verbally and non-verbally.

Expressing too much emotion can be overwhelming to people you live and work with – and it can impede your success. This was a concept I didn't fully understand when I was younger: I didn't know how to appropriately contain my emotions. Strong emotions were like hot potatoes: I had to get rid of them as quickly as possible. I often felt pressured to hurry up and tell my story or express my emotions. I'd actually gush with emotion. Perhaps this overlapped with inadequate impulse control, since people often told me I talked too much. As I developed my own emotional intelligence skills, I learned my strong emotional expressions hadn't always been appropriate to the situation.

You might relate to this story. When I was a CPA in public accounting, my boss told me I didn't behave like a "typical CPA" during my year-end review. This happened to me at different firms, and I don't think this was meant to be a compliment. Sometimes I was told I socialized in the office too much, smiled too much or acted too happy. I was also asked to comport myself in a more serious manner to gain respect and credibility in my field. The idea was CPAs should be quiet and keep their heads down. At the time, I didn't understand my chatty, open behavior didn't build trustworthiness and didn't earn the esteem of my peers in the financial services industry. Has something like this ever happened to you in the workplace?

Where it did come in handy, though, was when I engaged in business development. My natural emotional expressiveness wasn't appropriate for that particular work environment, but it was clearly an asset in helping build prospective client relationships. And, it was one of the building blocks to developing my interpersonal relationship skills.

I encountered this lack of skill in emotional expression again when I was pursuing my degree in marriage and family therapy. I was just beginning practicum, the year I started applying the cognitive knowledge I had learned in the classroom in working with real clients. My new supervisor was concerned that my bubbly, enthusiastic personality style might be "too much" for some clients. She thought I might overwhelm them. Just as in my experience as a CPA, I didn't receive this information well. My feelings were hurt and I was angry, though I didn't express that to my supervisor.

Growing up in my family, my parents discouraged children expressing anger, so I learned to suppress it. Only years later did I develop the freedom in myself to express anger appropriately. Of course, since my supervisor never knew I was hurt or angry, we never addressed the situation. I held in my feelings, which further hindered my emotional well-being and my progress in practicum. Looking back, I see how it would have been extremely helpful if my supervisor offered me advice on how to manage, contain and appropriately express emotions, especially those usually considered negative. Of course, that wasn't a workplace supervisor's job, so I asked for help from another source.

When I became fully conscious I had issues around emotion short-circuiting my professional success if I didn't resolve them, I consulted a Jungian analyst. To begin developing the skill of appropriate emotional expression, he encouraged me to draw, using expressive arts therapy. One day during our work together, I drew hot pink, red and orange images to show how I imagined my emotions looked when I expressed them openly – scattered, not contained. Interestingly, I chose blue and green to illustrate how I experienced emotions held in a vessel or other container – in other words, emotions I managed appropriately.

These images percolated in my unconscious mind while our talking sessions worked on my conscious mind. This was our routine: I'd tell my analyst about circumstances and situations that triggered my strong emotions and how I'd handled them – or not. I was so detail-oriented that I laid out every thread of the story for his perusal. He'd give me feedback, allowing me to see whether or not I had handled my emotions appropriately, given the situation.

If I hadn't, he offered examples of how I could have dealt with them more effectively, and expressed myself more appropriately. We were a good team, and I learned through this method over time how to use my emotions in the most productive way for the best results. This method also improved my impulse control and reality testing skills.

My process with clients is similar, only we use words, instead of art: They bring me challenging examples from their work life, and through a process of sifting and sorting, I help them see the situation more clearly and often from a higher perspective. As a result, my clients develop a stronger sense of motivation and conviction, rendering them more productive and efficient.

A short time ago, I met a client, Stacy, who reminded me of how I used to behave. Although she worked in a very conservative work environment, her casual demeanor and self-presentation didn't reflect her buttoned-up company culture. Even though she was highly skilled with a long history at the company, her boss told me she wasn't fully respected by her colleagues. Her mostly male coworkers didn't respond well to her emotional, chatty approach and didn't take her work seriously. Her boss wanted to help her develop a more sophisticated, corporate presence, which would allow her to be more effective in her role, so he contacted me to coach her.

Stacy's Story

Stacy was a 50-year-old woman from California who dressed like she was still in college. With pale skin and blonde hair, she was a petite woman, barely 5' tall in heels. Stacy was crazy about car racing – in fact, her boyfriend was a racecar driver. She spent all her free time at the racetracks following his career.

When I first met Stacy, I was struck by the intensity of her passion for her work at an accounting firm. She was every bit as driven as her male counterparts, and I wanted to help her earn their complete respect. The major difference I saw between her comportment and theirs was her casual, chatty style, which I suspected they dismissed as girly and naïve. In truth, this strong, competent and resilient woman was anything but that. She had successfully raised and parented a son by herself while working her way up in the company full-time for 30 years. Without having a college diploma, I knew this took true grit on her part to achieve and admired her strength.

Stacy was a warm, supportive person, and it was easy to connect with her. Although some people might feel threatened when their boss asks them to work with an executive coach, she wasn't and eagerly agreed to take the EQ-i 2.0 assessment. She was interested in doing whatever she could to develop her EQ-i 2.0 skills to increase her influence and visibility within the company. Her lack of resistance made her very easy to work with, as she was open to all of my suggestions.

The Evaluation

When deciding whether to take on a client, I assess their coachability first. To have a successful working relationship, the client must be open to outside feedback and want to improve their skills. In addition, it's helpful when they're cooperative and collaborative. In trying to predict the degree of coachability before starting work with a new person, I determine their eligibility based on three EQ-i 2.0 skills: self-regard, self-actualization and flexibility. If the prospective client scores high in all three, he or she usually makes a good candidate. Although we'd need to increase her self-regard in order to bring her into better balance, Stacy scored high in all of these skills, making her an excellent candidate.

Here's the process I followed, which is typical of how I work. After I gave Stacy the EQ-i 2.0 assessment, her overall EQ-i 2.0 score was in the mid-range. In the Self-Perception Composite, she was fairly balanced in the sub-scales, because none of the scores were more than 10 points apart. However, her scores in the Self-Expression Composite, which we're learning about in this section, were dramatically out of balance, with low-lows and high-highs.

For example, Stacy scored very high in emotional expression, very low in assertiveness and somewhat average in independence. These scores meant she wasn't operating effectively in the Self-Expression Composite. The same pattern was true in the next three composites: She was out of balance, again, with low-lows and high-highs, in the Interpersonal Composite, the Decision-Making Composite and the Stress Management Composite.

Next, I interviewed Stacy and her boss separately to further assess test validity and compare the results. Although this particular assessment instrument is quite robust when it comes to scientific reliability and validation (it assesses inconsistency and consistency, positive and negative impressions, and response distribution), best practices dictate thoroughly debriefing the person when delivering the report. Since no self-report is infallible or completely accurate, it's a best practice to ask the person if she thinks the results are what she expected and if there were any surprises. I always remind clients this report is a snapshot in time.

As such, it's a starting point for discussion and not the end of an investigation. When I asked Stacy if she thought her results were accurate, she agreed they were. To get additional feedback, I talked with her coworkers and peers; they all saw her as too emotionally expressive, impulsive and unaware of the impact of her vocal tones when she was conveying information. As a result, she didn't engender respect for her position in the company as well as she could have.

The Work

As Stacy and I began to work together, I made recommendations about how she could monitor her voice, modulating tone and volume to adjust to specific situations. I also suggested being mindful of facial expressions because she displayed emotions on her face very easily. "You don't have to go to the other extreme of having a poker face and showing no emotion at all," I told her, "but dialing down some of your expressions will help you convey more emotional authority."

We also talked about counting to 10 before speaking or responding to a situation to slow down her thought process. "Wow, when I try this, other people perceive me as being more in control," Stacy reported back to me.

"Right, responding thoughtfully instead of impulsively reacting will make a major difference in your personal communication style and help you create a much more favorable impression," I explained.

One of the things I learned from her boss was that Stacy needed to work more independently, with less need for guidance and reassurance from her. She said Stacy interrupted her too often, asking for help on things she thought she had given sufficient attention to previously. This made sense to me and validated her report results: Stacy's independence score was lower than her emotional expression score. In addition, she wanted her to take more initiative in moving assigned projects forward, without having to prompt her to make things happen. Her comments here also validated what showed on her report: She scored very low in assertiveness.

When working with Stacy on her independence skills, I probed deeper to isolate what caused her to rely too heavily on her boss's opinions. "Demonstrating independence means you're capable of thinking, feeling and working on your own without much need for reassurance from others," I told her.

One of the things I discovered was that Stacy's ability to use her independence skills was inconsistent and situational. "When I feel very comfortable, I rely on my own opinion, make decisions and move forward on my own," she said. However in other situations, such as when she worried her opinion was different from either the group consensus or her boss's, she was concerned she'd be judged.

We discussed how Stacy would benefit from building this skill and using it consistently in a variety of contexts. We agreed increased independence would equip her to take appropriate risks, provide direction to her team and make firm decisions even when others might disagree with her.

Since her boss preferred she make more decisions on her own without consulting her first, we worked on Stacy's ability to develop firm conviction for the direction she chose to take. One of the directives I gave her was to form the habit of listing pros and cons in her journal. I suggested that before she make a decision or take action, she list out and weigh both the positive and negative reactions her boss and her team might have regarding her course of action.

By anticipating and thinking through these possible reactions beforehand, listing them out and then listening to people's reactions afterward, Stacy would eventually be in a position to predict them ahead of time. By having her well-documented script of why she made certain choices, she'd feel sure of herself and be able to convey her feelings and thoughts from a stronger stance. Stacy adopted this methodology and was pleased to see how list making and documenting her thought process quickly became a habit. "Doing this makes me feel less anxious and more prepared," she told me.

I also helped Stacy become more aware of the moments when she wanted reassurance from her boss. I asked her to stop herself before going to her office or writing an e-mail to consult her. Instead, I asked her to take out her journal and write down what she was thinking and questioning. I asked her to imagine how her conversation might go with the boss and either write it out or outline it in bullet points.

Then I asked her to study it from her boss's perspective. What might she be thinking or feeling while listening to her? Would she welcome the conversation or regard it as an unnecessary interruption? Is there something more she could flesh out on her own or is the next step truly dependent on her boss's authority?

Next, I asked her to think about this from a meta-level point of view by taking this up a level and considering it from a higher perspective.

Looking at the bigger picture, what did the situation look like then? Did consulting her boss at this particular moment suit her role and central purpose for her work, or not?

At this point in our time together, one of the things we did was go back and formulate Stacy's vision for her role as a leader in her company. Starting with her job description and moving past that to her own sense of what she wanted to accomplish in her role, we formulated a statement of her vision. We referred to this as her central purpose for being a leader in the company. We cross-referenced this document with the vision her boss had for her work, to make certain they were compatible and congruent.

Then I asked her to consistently communicate from this central vision and to come back to it always, without getting distracted by irrelevant small talk or focusing on sidebar conversations. I asked her to think of her independence as riding on this central vision, because then her listeners would be captivated and her influence would increase. Indeed, her team started to take Stacy more seriously and listen to her more intently after she began following this practice and incorporating it into her daily routine.

The Results

The culture Stacy worked in was very competitive, where most of her coworkers, including her boss, were more assertive than her. To address the big picture and be more effective, she had to build skills in this area, too.

Independence and assertiveness go hand-in-hand. To think for yourself, make your own decisions and execute plans without the need for others' assurance, you also need to find your voice and use it. This is problematic if you don't know what your voice is saying to you. Since Stacy scored well in emotional self-awareness, she already heard and knew her own voice. She just had to practice using it, especially in workplace situations where there were a lot of differing opinions.

I helped Stacy understand the difference between being too passive by not offering her opinion at all or not taking any initiative and being too aggressive by attempting to control other people and insisting her way is best without considering their point of view. I helped her understand being assertive is a behavior right in the middle of the two extremes. It involves creating a situation for both parties so they each feel like winners.

Stacy practiced having courageous conversations instead of confrontations. By this time, she had already improved her skills at processing, containing and managing her own emotions so she was very successful at embracing and enhancing this one last skill. As she did so, her Self-Expression Composite became better balanced: She earned her colleagues' respect by being able to effectively express her thoughts and feelings, and taking action on work projects autonomously.

Building Your Emotional Expression

We all experience emotions every moment of every day. Yet, we all operate at different levels of emotional expression. You may be hyper-aware of your emotions and either hide them from others or have them written all over your face. You may even choose to display an emotion that's different from what you're actually feeling. You might be thinking, "It's better not to share my true emotions with people, especially at work. It's safer that way." However, what if there's a balance? What if skillful emotional expression is essential to being successful in your workplace as a leader, as a sales manager, as a teammate?

If you interview a job candidate, what if the person won't make steady eye contact with you or smile? Do you interpret that as the person just being nervous, or do you immediately think, "This person is unfriendly. He won't fit in here." Or what if you spent a week working on a report for your client, and when you handed it to her, she starts reading it, and then looks up with a slight smile on her lips that doesn't show in her eyes and says flatly, "Great. Thanks." How does that make you feel? Probably that she's not very impressed with your work, since her words don't match the obvious body language, which as humans, we're attuned to picking up.

Similarly, your boss, coworkers, direct reports, and family and friends watch you for similar signals. If the emotions you express match what they predict and expect, they'll trust you more, even if they don't necessarily like the emotion because they know it's authentic. No one wants to play emotional guessing games, especially at work or with prospects and clients. When someone expresses inauthentic emotions, other people's responses are to avoid you, because your behavior makes them feel confused and anxious.

Emotional expression is essential to boost our well-being and self-acceptance. When you regularly hide your emotions, you're hiding parts of who you are. You might even feel guilty or ashamed, which will only further tarnish your self-regard and confidence. That leads to negative self-talk: "There must be something wrong with me because I have to hide the true me. But if they knew the true me they wouldn't like me or think I'm good at my job." In addition, if you get in the habit of hiding emotions from others, you're likely hiding them from yourself as well, making it harder for you to make the best decisions for you.

And of course, skillful emotional expression requires that you know when and how to display your emotions. Going to the other extreme where you express every feeling in an over-the-top way reads as immature to others. Expressing real emotions in a mature, self-assured way sparks respect, trust and cooperation in others.

Let's return to the example of your client reading your report. Let's say she read it with a serious expression, and then looked up and said, "Good start, but it still needs some additional work. Want to brainstorm?" While this may not be the reaction you want, your client is displaying authentic emotions and matching feedback. You have a true starting point for meaningful dialogue, a mutually beneficial outcome and a relationship based on respect and trust.

Exercises for Exploration and Mastery: Emotional Expression

I work with many people who've either shut down their emotions completely or revved them up beyond normal. Let's start with an exercise I often use for clients who fit those circumstances.

Exercise 1

Get a pocket notebook you can easily carry around with you. Set an intention to pick three set times during the day when you'll stop to reflect and jot down notes in your book. When you do this, notice your circumstances and what's going on around you. For example, you could write that you just stopped to get gas for your car. Next, write down the situation, circumstances or something specific that's happening. You could say that just as you pulled into the station, someone cut you off at the gas pump. Now write down your emotional response to the situation. You could say you were angry; on a scale of 1-10, you were an eight within two seconds.

Your Takeaway: Do this exercise daily, and you'll start to notice your emotional behavior patterns.

Exercise 2

Now, take this first exercise a step further. Can you identify what's really underneath the surface of what triggered you? Was it really the situation you were in, or did that remind you of something that happened to you in the past?

Your Takeaway: Learning to see patterns will help you identify situations from your past that you can change for your future.

Exercise 3

Let's take these first two exercises further. Practice emotional expression with a trusted friend, spouse, partner or coach. Using your pocket notebook from Exercise 1, read it out loud to the person you chose. Ask them to give you feedback about your emotional expression. For example, did they notice what you were feeling by watching your face, tone of voice, body language and so on?

Your Takeaway: Consider whether the emotion you displayed was congruent with what you felt.

Exercise 4

Practice feeling vulnerable. If you're a leader, or aspire to be one, a Towers Perrin Global Workforce Study (2007-2008), indicated employees are more engaged in their work when their senior management is sincerely interested in employee well-being, when they communicate openly and honestly, when they attempt to be visible and accessible, when they communicate the reasons for key business decisions, and when their actions are consistent with their values. Take a moment and rate yourself. How do think you do when it comes to these key elements? Which ones are you best at and which do you need to improve?

Your Takeaway: Make a strategic plan to work on those you need to improve and stick to your plan daily.

Exercise 5

Find your sweet spot between being too vulnerable and too closed off. By working with the tension of these opposites, you'll land in your perfect place between feeling too exposed and hiding your feelings. If you think you disclose too much of your personal life and feelings to your coworkers or boss, how could you take a small step back? What do you think the consequences or benefits of that small step back would be? If you think you close yourself off like a fortress, try sharing something small and personal with your coworkers or boss. Notice any consequences or benefits that ensue.

Your Takeaway: Repeat this practice daily, going back and forth, until you find that sweet spot where you feel comfortable and notice that others respond to you in appropriate ways. Perhaps they'll feel more connected to you now.

Story Two: Tom

independence: the ability to be self-directed and self-controlled in your thinking and actions and be free of emotional dependency.
assertiveness: the ability to express feelings, beliefs, and thoughts, and defend your rights in a nondestructive manner.

Many readers will nod in agreement as they're reading this chapter: Most of us personally and professionally have difficulty building our assertiveness, because we confuse it with aggressiveness. In addition, it's often hard for us to act confident – clear and steady in our convictions – especially when we live and work with people who'll usually have differing opinions than us, and we don't want to appear difficult or like we're pointing out that a differing opinion is incorrect.

You know that when you act a certain way, your behavior sends a message to those around you. Let's break down three behavioral options you have when faced with conflict – aggressiveness, assertiveness and passivity – and how others might perceive those.

Let's start with aggression. At work, imagine your boss grumbles, "I want the deal closed by the end of the day, or you're off this team." Or what if you asked an employee to spend some extra time on a project, and he retorts, "There's no way I'm staying late tonight to work on this!" The underlying aggressive message that's heard in either case is: "If you get in my way, I'll make things hard for you!"

Conversely, passivity communicates, "You can do whatever you want to me because I'll do whatever it takes to avoid conflict." A friend or coworker who says things like, "Go ahead, you pick what doughnut you want. I'll take whatever's left," or "I had dinner plans tonight, but if you want me to stay late to work on this project I'll cancel them." Unfortunately, though, way too many people react passively, because they mistake acting assertively with aggression, and this becomes a pattern of behavior.

Assertiveness, however, is expressing your needs and wants in a polite, respectful way that communicates reciprocity like this: "Each of our needs is important, and we're going to work together to achieve what's needed without hurting each other." Being assertive isn't just something you do when you're having a conflict with someone; it's a skill that helps you act in agreeance and avoid conflict. Returning to the earlier example of a grumbling boss, what if he says, "We really need to close that deal today. What can I do to help make that happen?" Your reaction would be totally different, and you'd likely be willing to go the extra mile to make it happen.

When you're a non-assertive team leader, you may not tell your staffers specifically what you want them to do and by when. Then when they don't achieve their goals, you fume silently or complain to them about their job performance. Your team feels hurt and then isn't motivated to perform at all. However, when you're an assertive boss, you clearly identify your goals and talk with your staff constructively about their specific roles and tasks to move toward those end results.

Here's one key to understanding assertiveness: Think of it on a continuum, from passivity, including passive aggression, to all-out aggression. Neither extreme is effective. Ideally, you want to land on that sweet spot in the middle, where you help negotiate a win-win situation for both parties, and create a relationship of solid trust. In addition, assertiveness is also a posture of taking initiative and right action.

As far as independence in a workplace, you can struggle with expressing your opinion either because if you dissent from the group, you feel like you're not conforming or perhaps pointing out the group's error. There are clearly times for independence and dependence at work. You know that sometimes in meetings, everyone gets lulled into group think and might need that one lone voice to change things up.

Other times, you might need to modify or let go of your perceptions either because you're wrong or there are several right answers, and the group's decision really is best in that instance. The key is in learning when to be independent and when to trust others' judgement, in addition to trusting your own inner judgement vs. needing too much reassurance from others that your ideas are on point.

When I first met Tom, I immediately felt comfortable with him. He was smart and presented himself in a quiet, unassuming manner: There was no hubris when dealing with him. He was easy to talk to and very open about his personal and career struggles. He espoused old-fashioned family values and had a big heart for his family's physical, financial and spiritual well-being – and that touched me. Tom was also very dedicated to caring for everyone in his orbit, including coworkers, fellow church members and neighbors. When I talked with Tom, I suspected this dedication was holding him back, making his greatest strength his greatest liability.

Tom's Story

Tom was a 42-year-old, blue-eyed blonde from northern Iowa. He was a Wartburg grad, and a master chess player. He was very good at mathematics. Strong and stocky, his presence filled the room when he entered it.

Tom's EQ-i 2.0 workplace report revealed he scored highest on social responsibility, more than 10 points out of balance with his next highest score, a tie for empathy and impulse control. Think of this as having a very high level of patience, almost to the point of being too tolerable. This affected Tom's career performance negatively, for example, because he put others' needs and problems so far ahead of his own that he risked achieving his own professional goals.

Now let's look at the negative side of impulse control: Tom was so patient, coworkers perceived him as lacking a sense of urgency because he didn't seem to react quickly enough. What they didn't know, however, was Tom was indeed reacting, albeit internally. His reaction was to mull everything over, thinking things through again and again to the point of paralysis by analysis. His self-doubt and lack of emotional self-awareness caused him to labor too long at making important decisions; sometimes this left him benched on the sidelines and out of the game.

Tom's lowest EQ-i 2.0 scores were in the Self-Expression Composite and this further exacerbated his high and out-of-balance scores in impulse control and social responsibility.

Think of it this way: Imagine how laid-back a person might seem if he's overly patient, caring and non-assertive. How would you respond? You'd think he's kind, but you'd overlook his ability to make a significant contribution in a fast-paced, competitive workplace. I wanted to help Tom increase these specific EQ-i 2.0 skills because he was smart and technically competent, and if he did he'd help a lot of people through his job as a mortgage loan officer. He was approachable and he could connect with prospective clients easily without seeming like a pushy salesperson.

Tom was stopped at a crossroads because it was hard for him to decide whether he could really do his job and make this his lifelong career. He was well-liked at his firm and although everyone was cheering him on, from the managing partner on down, he had trouble absorbing and owning their encouragement. Until he believed in himself and his ability to succeed at this career and do it well, he was always at cross-purposes: his passion for his work vs. his lack of faith in himself.

The Evaluation

Since Tom's production was low and his impulse control was high, I felt a terrific sense of urgency to help him ramp up his activity. One of the first exercises I assigned him was to review all the reasons he entered his field. This assignment seemed fairly easy for him, and here's what he identified as his passions for being in the business:

> I want to be productive and help people.
>
> I want to help my family by providing for them financially.
>
> I enjoy being able to contribute financially to my church.
>
> I like the feeling of teamwork and camaraderie that exists at my firm.
>
> I'm motivated by the freedom to make my own choices and I like working for myself.
>
> I want to make my family proud of me.

When Tom and I reviewed this list he said, "I don't understand why I can't get out there and knock on more doors so I can get new clients!" When we examined the reasons for this, Tom revealed a common fear: He didn't want to get on the phone and face more rejection. "I keep blaming myself for not taking action and moving forward," he told me.

This was how his low skill in assertiveness, which is about initiative and taking action, affected his emotional expression. In other words, if

Tom lacked conviction in his own authority, it would be hard for him to convey a confident, competent attitude to a potential client.

Since Tom also scored low in self-regard, I designed homework exercises to help him build his confidence and assertiveness. One of the ways to build positive attitude is to use words of affirmation, both verbal and written, to create change in both the unconscious and conscious minds. Since Tom was disappointed in himself and felt he was letting others down (he also admitted thinking he was a "stupid loser who didn't deserve to have a good life"), I wrote this positive affirmation for him to use: "I'm a trusted advisor."

I requested he write it down in his journal over and over again, and memorize it and say it to himself as often as possible, like when he's in the shower, driving, brushing his teeth, falling asleep or waking up. When we're doing mundane or routine tasks, those are the times we have the easiest access to our unconscious mind because the conscious is distracted. I also suggested he read the book *Feel the Fear and Do It Anyway* by Susan Jeffers.

A week later I asked Tom to write down his responses to the following: "I want to be successful in order to ...." One of his most practical responses was to "pay the bills" and the other was more emotional in nature: "so I won't be rejected." I encouraged Tom to take action without worrying about whether everything else is perfect because he over-researched before taking action. It was another form of paralysis by analysis. You could also say his fear and doubts caused him to procrastinate.

To inspire Tom, I shared three things I've learned about barriers to moving forward and conquering defeatist self-thinking:

- If you just do one thing that stretches you past your comfort zone everyday (even if it isn't the breakthrough item you committed to), you set yourself up for future success.

- Sometimes the item you committed to isn't what your soul wants you to do right now. Sometimes something else has to happen first or be in place before you can take the planned action, when there's more room in your psyche.

- Consistency and perseverance are key to establishing forward movement, in addition to your belief in a higher power or a cause greater than yourself. Your motivation must come from within.

The Work

For Tom to understand I personally "got" his reluctance to take action, I shared that my biggest stretch has always been to believe in myself. Growing up, my mother used to tell me regularly that I was dumb and couldn't figure things out by myself. When I spoke my opinion, she told me I was crazy or had it all wrong. I've worked with several therapists and coaches to change this pattern. In certain contexts, if I'm not mindful of my thoughts and emotions, I can still fall into this negative thinking trap. At times it can stop me from taking initiative and being assertive. Tom was struggling with similar demons, and I wanted to help him break free.

Actually, almost everyone I've worked with has their own version of this story: It's whatever that thing is holding you back from accomplishing what you want and need to do. Often, clients tell me the same thing: They know what they need to do, but the problem is that they don't know why they just don't do it. James Hollis, a Jungian analyst whose thoughts I value, says we all suffer from some version of anxiety, overwhelm or lethargy internalized through our ego's self-negating voice. Instead of listening to the ego, Hollis suggests we follow our soul's voice, which would always lead us to play a more active game and take on a larger role in life. To do that, you need to drive down from the top through cognitive behavioral exercises and simultaneously build up from the bottom through activation of your unconscious. Both types of exercises are necessary to create long-lasting change.

I floated my hypothesis by Tom, and we had several meetings where we discussed and dissected unhappy events that happened while growing up in his family. I was correct in my hypothesis: Tom's mother suffered from anxiety, depression and mental illness that caused her to be very critical of her children. "No matter what I did I couldn't please my mother," Tom told me, this reflecting his high social responsibility score. During our work together, all kinds of childhood memories surfaced for Tom. "Until now, I didn't realize my low self-regard was influenced by these events," he said. "It makes me feel better to know there's a valid reason for all of my negative self-talk. I absorbed it unconsciously from my mother."

Despite inheriting this negative self-talk and his struggles with emotional swings, Tom was actually very successful. He held a SAFE license and a mortgage loan officer (MLO) certification.

Tom's low score in emotional expression might explain his mood swings. As suggested in Tom's workplace report, people who score low in this skill have difficulty bringing emotions to the surface and sharing their true feelings with coworkers. This may cause them to appear emotionally detached from colleagues because they show as little variation in their demeanor as possible. This is called having a flat affect.

The EQ-i 2.0 report results urged Tom to consider the following as characteristic of himself: Certain emotions, if not most, are uncomfortable for you to express either through words, facial expressions or body language. You use a limited emotional vocabulary to describe your feelings, like happy and sad vs. elated and somber. You assume people know how you feel, so you don't display it through your words or actions.

In addition, Tom was used to bottling up his emotions and feelings so he appeared expressionless at work. Combining this with his low score in assertiveness, it was easy to see why he came across as passive. Coworkers assumed he didn't have a sense of urgency when needed or that he failed to grasp the significance of important situations.

The same assessment report urged Tom to think about his emotions as performance drivers, just like any other resource he could draw upon to get his job done. What we did in our work together was to use his family environment as a practice ground. Since Tom had such strong family ties and values, I suggested he spend more time socializing on the weekends with his wife, children, extended family, neighbors and church friends whenever possible. His wife assisted him in this endeavor, and they started inviting more people over on the weekends.

I suggested Tom start slowly by taking appropriate steps to express and share his feelings at these weekend gatherings because they represented a space where he felt very comfortable. This really seemed to help him cultivate a more expressive face, including appropriately reflective body language, and he began to have fun and relax while socializing. In addition, this helped fill up his emotional tank for the start of the next week.

We also addressed Tom's low assertiveness score: He was seen as a team player, supportive of everyone else, but passive when it came to standing up for his own beliefs. In meetings, Tom was labeled an observer rather than a participant. Even though he had extensive knowledge and valuable experience to share, Tom had trouble articulating his opinions and feelings, so he kept them to himself. Because of this, he wasn't able to convey his genuine passion or enthusiasm and didn't come across as engaged and committed to the team.

Many of Tom's fears about speaking up could be traced to his childhood experiences. As a child, speaking up to his mother had negative consequences and as an adult he was afraid the same thing would happen now if he spoke his true opinion in team meetings. One of the things that helped him start changing his mind was to brainstorm a list of negative consequences that had already occurred as a result of withholding opinions and not expressing true feelings at work.

Then we discussed how long the same list would be if he continued to refrain from asserting himself: one year, three years, five years, 10 years and 20 years down the road. It was a long list. Then we made a list of positive consequences that would result from Tom taking initiative, and communicating a clear stand. I was happy to show Tom this one was the longest list, and he used it to motivate himself to start taking action.

Here are some questions I asked Tom to answer in his journal and share with me later:

- What does winning professionally look like to you? Define your answer as specifically as possible and include metrics so we can measure your success by number of new clients, increased loan volume production, higher credit quality scores, and a higher percentage of client retention. Identify the numbers you'd have to reach for you to feel like you won this quarter, and this year.

- Describe what it would look like or feel like when you're focused on accepting personal, professional and financial responsibility for where you are in your life and career.

- Decide what steps you can take to change your current reality if you're unhappy with it.

- In what ways are your doubts and fears influencing your procrastination? Upon reflection, do you think these doubts and fears are valid or are they over-exaggerated? Think of a situation that took place in the past week where you behaved passively. Write down the thoughts that went through your mind and held you back from behaving assertively. Looking back, what were the negative consequences you imagined might happen if you behaved assertively? What did you learn from this experience that might help you behave more assertively in the future?

- Think of a scenario in which you behaved assertively in the past week. What were the thoughts and feelings that accompanied your being assertive? What were the positive consequences of taking action?

The Results

As a result of doing his homework, Tom became more energized and started taking more risks, including making his prospecting phone calls. As he started seeing more success as a result of his efforts, he realized he felt more positive. This realization brought up more fearful insights from his unconscious, such as the idea he was more afraid of being rejected, not liked or not accepted than being hit by a two-by-four. He'd be able to challenge people about doing what it takes to achieve their financial goals if he didn't care so much about being liked and accepted. He also said his parents never trusted anyone who was a salesperson and he didn't want to be seen as pushy. Since Tom had access to clients with several million dollars in assets and needed to challenge them to move forward on their goals, we reframed these thoughts so he could think of himself as "persistent, but polite," and this worked well for him.

Tom often asked me, "How do I convince myself I'm just as good as everyone else?" I suggested he think about being strong and courageous, and attempt to convey that to clients through his body language and tone of voice whenever he met with them. "I'm learning to promote myself as an expert, trusted advisor," Tom said. He was starting to understand he really liked to work and that the more activity he did like phone calls and meetings, the better he felt about himself. Tom was taking more consistent action, and it was self-generating and starting to pay off. He noticed he had stopped over-thinking things before executing tasks. This was a valuable new awareness for him.

At the end of our time together, we went back to the beginning and looked at his original reasons for why he was passionate about his industry. He decided to add something to the list: his love of helping people. He told me that even though making a lot of money meant he helped a lot of people, it wasn't a motivator for him. His true motivation came from helping others, including his family, serving his church and community, and the money followed as a by-product. He really liked the idea that the more money he made, the more he could contribute to his family and favorite charities. "I'm a pretty decent person," Tom told me at the end of our time together. "I have a handful of things I need to change and re-evaluate, and I need to be as emotionally tough as I'm physically tough, yet I'm pretty good. I'm still making improvements in my emotional intelligence."

His appointments, new clients and loans under management had increased, and a local chapter of the National Association of Mortgage

Brokers had honored him with a service recognition award.

Building Your Independence and Assertiveness

Let's review. You've learned that assertiveness in both your personal and professional lives will serve you well. Think back to a time when you acted aggressively, say raising your voice, when you perceived someone was disrespecting you. Consider how you felt afterward and how the other person reacted. It's important to note that sometimes when we perceive that someone else is disrespecting or trying to dominate us, we give ourselves permission to act in kind. However, sometimes our perceptions are incorrect because of our own irrational thoughts or because we don't fully know what's going on with others, leading us to misread their intentions.

If your job requires you to manage employees or work with coworkers, vendors and clients, you want to master the art of the win-win negotiation, where you work to help each other get what they what and need. Assertiveness is a key skill because you're able to clearly articulate how you need the other party to help you achieve your win.

As we learned early in this chapter, independence and dependence both have a role in workplace relationships. Sometimes, you might be the lone person in a group to present a differing point of view, and break your teammates out of groupthink. Other times, you might need to let go of a particular opinion because there are several right answers, and the group consensus about going with another idea might be best. The key is knowing when to be independent and when to trust your boss, team and staffers.

Exercises for Exploration and Mastery: Independence and Assertiveness

An important trait of assertive people is that they're poised to achieve their goals because they've taken the time to reflect and think things through. By making this effort they've achieved a degree of clarity and can communicate their wants, beliefs and feelings to others in a clear and unambiguous way, while taking into account and considering other's viewpoints.

As a result of this clarity, assertive people stand their ground when others offer resistance. The secret sauce to their success is their ability to articulate what they desire and to be transparent in communicating where they stand, while at the same time being respectful of others' needs

If you take the time to achieve this degree of clarity, you'll be able to articulate what you want, what you believe and how you feel in a succinct way. You'll have achieved a higher degree of self-awareness. This will set you up for success, and others will want to help you achieve your goals.

In a similar way, achieving this degree of clarity will also help you be appropriately independent. When you have firm conviction in your own ideas, beliefs and viewpoints, meaning you know exactly what they are and why you have them, you're often emboldened in taking the steps necessary to carry them out despite resistance from others. In a sense, you're also less vulnerable to being swayed off course by the influence of others who oppose your point of view. Instead, you're an advocate for the facts as well as for your opinions. You can stand firm and steadfast when you need to, yet you can be open to other right courses of action. You're free from emotional dependency, and you're self-directed.

Now, work through these exercises below in order, if you can, to obtain the full benefits of this section.

Exercise 1

What does winning professionally and being successful mean to you? Be specific. Define your answer in terms of your passions, beliefs and convictions.

Exercise 2

Describe what it would look like or feel like when you're focused on accepting personal, professional and financial responsibility for where you are in your life and career. How will you change your reality if you're currently unhappy with where you are now?

Exercise 3

Think of a situation that took place in the past week in which you behaved passively. Write down the thoughts that went through your mind (the negative self-talk) that controlled your thinking and interfered with you behaving assertively. Looking back, what were you concerned might happen if you behaved assertively? How did you expect the other person might react if you had asserted yourself?

Exercise 4

Think of a situation in the past week where you behaved too aggressively. Write down the thoughts and feelings you experienced at the time. How did the other person react?

Exercise 5

Think of a scenario in which you behaved assertively in the past week. What were the thoughts and feelings that accompanied your being assertive? How did the other person react?

Exercise 6

At times, we all behave in passive ways dependent on other people's thinking and not our own. Can you identify a time this week when that happened? If so, what was your internal dialogue at the time? We all have irrational thoughts. What were yours in this scenario? Map them out and see what irrational thoughts that held you hostage.

Exercise 7

Examine your behavior from a meta-level to identify patterns and scenarios in which you lose your sense of self-direction and rely too much on other's opinions. Now do the reverse, and see where you step out and set the trend. What do these scenarios have in common? How are they different? Is there any part of your mindset that needs to change or improve? If so, how will you take next steps to achieve that?

Your Takeaway: Remember, there isn't only one way of being assertive: Everyone has his or her own style. You can be humorous or serious, concise or elegant. We aren't all the same.

The ability to act with a proper degree of assertiveness breaks down in three ways:

- You must have sufficient self-awareness to recognize feelings before you express them.

- You must have sufficient impulse control and emotional expression to express disapproval and even anger without letting it escalate into fury. This means you can express a range of desires in the appropriate way with the appropriate intensity.

- Finally, you must stand up for your own rights, your own causes and deeply held beliefs, both to yourself and to others.

This means being able to disagree with others without resorting to emotional sabotage or subterfuge, and being able to walk a fine line, defending your wishes while at the same time respecting another person's point of view and being sensitive to their needs. This often results in constructive compromise, or a win-win situation because the bonds of a relationship are strengthened when both parties show consideration, and both are likely to walk away with their needs at least partially met.

Part III

Interpersonal Composite

Story One: Victor

interpersonal relationships: the ability to establish
and maintain mutually satisfying relationships
characterized by intimacy and by giving and receiving
affection.

Let's say you operate at a sales role in your company, and your manager
changes the team's quota structure so all of a sudden you have to close
more deals before the quarter ends. You're about to give a presentation
to a big, potential client, but you're experiencing major butterflies and
a racing heart. You approach a coworker who's making coffee and blurt
out, "I'm nervous about this presentation today! I really need to close
this deal, and I'm going over and over all the client's objections in my
head."

In scene one, your coworker shakes his head, saying saucily, "Oh, I
never get nervous! That's for amateurs." How would you feel? Rejected,
embarrassed and likely not to ever share your business-related emotions
with that person.

In scene two, this coworker chuckles in recognition, saying, "Yes, me
too! This new sales quota is tough to get used to. Want to hear a couple
things I do before I go on sales calls that pump me up?"

Knowing how to build appropriate relationships at work is so key,
and part of that is discussing emotions about business-related or shared
situations with your colleagues. This skill is especially important for
leaders who want to inspire their teams to build a certain type of corporate culture and work toward shared goals.

On a warm fall day, I read this message from Victor in my LinkedIn
mailbox: "Roberta, I'm the new CEO of a technology company. I've

recently taken on this leadership role and want to revamp my company culture using emotional intelligence principles as the basis for changing our core competencies. Let me know if you're interested in discussing this with me."

This was an exciting email to receive because I had already witnessed the efficacy of using emotional intelligence and interpersonal relationships to drive company culture in positive directions: It's possible to take a corporate mission statement, vision and core competencies and map them to the EQ-i 2.0 model. In this way, you can use EQ-i 2.0 principles to drive positive corporate culture, complete with resonant leadership and healthy employee engagement. In addition, I like the challenge of working with leaders transitioning into new roles and carving out new possibilities for their companies. The work is fulfilling, because both corporate and employee lives are touched by the transformation. For these reasons, I answered quickly and affirmatively to Victor's request.

At the core of what we worked on together was the ability to form positive interpersonal relationships, one of the most important factors in leadership and success in the workplace.

When you build positive relationships with others, obviously people will be more interested in following your lead, collaborating and encouraging others to work positively with you.

Let's look at two types of behaviors that create rock-solid relationships. First, exchanging emotionally intimate information creates trust and comfortability between people. Second, reciprocal affection, when you give and receive praise, works wonders: We all want to be liked.

Of course, exchanging intimate information and heaping on praise will be different with your spouse than with your coworkers and direct reports. It's important for you to know you can share relevant emotions with your colleagues. If you're nervous before a big sales presentation at a new client's office, it's totally appropriate for you to share that with a couple, trusted colleagues: They most likely will commiserate and may even offer some helpful tips. Likewise, telling a coworker you enjoy working with him and then complimenting his work on your latest project will go a long way toward building your relationship.

Victor's Story

Victor was a tall, 6'4" Texan who'd been transplanted to the Midwest. With red hair and cowboy boots underneath his suit, this Texas A&M graduate felt right at home in the corner office.

When I met Victor for the first time in his modern, beautifully decorated office in a busy commercial neighborhood, I was amazed by the magnitude of the project he had just accepted. The previous chief executive officer recently bolted from the company without two weeks' formal notice and no hand-picked successor to take the reins. Victor volunteered for the position and upper management approved. When Victor took over, the C-suite leadership team was in crisis and employee morale was at an all-time low.

In addition, the former leader, though financially successful, was an old-school curmudgeon: He ruled the office with an iron fist and a sour demeanor. Staffers worked long hours for below-market wages. Turnover was higher than market average, although surprisingly, many employees stayed. The former leader, though irritable when in a low mood, was charismatic and enigmatic when he was in a high mood. During those magnanimous times, he heaped on the praise and affirmation in a big way, and kept employees wanting more of his attention. Since his moods were inconsistent, though, employees never knew what response to expect; they'd hope his roller coaster of emotions would end, and he'd stay in a good mood.

When Victor took over, he wanted to change the culture he'd inherited and transform it into something healthier, for both the executive leadership team and employees. Although I realized Victor had his work cut out for him, I told him I wanted to help him move his vision forward and took the assignment. I knew employees would be skeptical of any new approach, because they didn't know who to trust or what to expect going forward. I also knew it was possible to change people's attitudes and company culture for the better by using EQ-i 2.0 principles.

One of the first things I did was interview Victor's direct reports. I asked them what was going well and what needed improvement, as well as how they felt about the former leader leaving and Victor taking over his position. What I learned didn't surprise me, because I could see some of what the employees saw reflected in my own experience when interacting with Victor. For example, Victor's voice was measured and flat, and he maintained a poker face, so he was incredibly hard to read.

Although he wasn't aware this was how his employees perceived him, his expressionlessness distanced them from him, since they could never guess how he viewed them and their performance. That translated into them being hesitant to trust him. Some staffers even saw his overly reserved demeanor as inauthentic, because they felt no one could be that well-guarded and still be empathetic.

I also learned Victor had incredibly high standards and expectations, both of himself and others. Although he held himself accountable to these same principles, his employees didn't pick up on this. They only saw and felt that they were being measured by impossibly high benchmarks, and they also wanted a good work-life balance, too. Victor was a hard worker and valued hard work from his team, as well.

I wasn't sure Victor or his team knew where to draw healthy boundaries. That's because the team tended to work 24/7, plus they socialized outside work and considered themselves friends. I didn't know where they drew the line between business and socializing or between work and play. They might always be strategizing about the next deal, with no downtime.

Some of the team missed the former leader's contagious charisma, though no one missed his erratic moods. The team was happy and content to have someone more emotionally predictable in his place, which was a positive thing. However, they wanted to feel their leader understood them, while guiding them and cheering them on. When Victor first took over as CEO, they didn't experience him as an empathetic, resonant leader. Instead, his direct reports described him as being rigid and unapproachable, rehearsed and not genuine, and that sometimes he shut down around them. This didn't seem to be the real Victor, and I hypothesized that underneath the guarded manner was a warm, generous and compassionate leader just waiting to be liberated from his past experiences.

The Evaluation

Once Victor completed the EQ-i 2.0 leadership assessment, we had a vehicle to deliver the results of my interviews as well as a geographically and professionally normed report. The report gave me a clear, structured way to share the results of my work thus far, and to help Victor see how his EQ-i 2.0 skills compared to that of other leaders, from mid-level management up through C-suite leaders, in a variety of different industries including healthcare, technology, financial services and construction located across North America.

In addition, the leadership report offered insight into Victor's strengths as well as potential areas for improvement, through four key dimensions of leadership: authenticity, coaching, insight and innovation. As a group, the average total emotional intelligence score for these leaders was 14 points higher than that of the general population. Many professionals achieve greater clarity by focusing on improving two or three specific skills underlying broader leadership competencies, rather than attempting to improve many different skills simultaneously. The EQ-i 2.0 subscales are the perfect building blocks to achieving full leadership potential.

Victor scored lower on his overall EQ-i 2.0 assessment than I would have anticipated from a leader. However, I knew the assessment results can be under-reported (usually by about 10 points, though the balancing patterns will usually be the same) when someone experiences an adjustment period or transition time, which was true in this case. Victor scored high in self-actualization, which meant he wanted to be the best leader he could possibly be, so his interest was hooked by this report. He immediately saw the value of working to increase his EQ-i 2.0 skills.

Victor had taken a bold step at this company when he switched gears from being a nationally recognized "top 10" technology salesperson to "starting over" again as senior vice president of sales, leading and motivating a team of commissioned salespeople to produce for him. Now he had taken on the role of CEO. In fact, this wasn't an easy switch

To become a Star Performer, Victor needed to develop new EQ-i 2.0 skills because these career positions called for two different EQ-i 2.0 skillsets, although there's some overlap. In my experience, the top three EQ-i 2.0 skills needed for Star Performer CEOs are empathy, self-regard and assertiveness. According to Steven J. Stein, Ph.D., and Howard E. Book, M.D., in their book *The EQ Edge: Emotional Intelligence and Your Success*, the top five skills for business salespeople are self-regard, reality testing, assertiveness, stress tolerance and optimism.

To engage his employees and redesign his corporate culture successfully, Victor needed to develop a Star Performer CEO's skills. In his case, he scored very high in assertiveness and low in empathy and flexibility. Since those scores differed by more than 10 points, the Bar-On Model considered him to be out of balance in those areas. In other words, he was taking action, or being assertive, without conveying enough warmth, or empathy, causing his direct reports to feel distant from him. He was also being assertive by taking action, but because he wasn't also looking at other legitimate courses of action, he displayed inflexibility. Some of Victor's team didn't want to change processes that worked for them, just because their CEO saw things differently. Conversely, Victor didn't understand why his team didn't want to follow the tried-and-true successful path he believed he was sharing with them.

Sometimes being high in one subscale, when not balanced by another, can actually hinder your success. Victor had challenges associated with high scores in two skills: self-actualization and assertiveness. According to the Bar-On Model, when some people score high in self-actualization without being balanced with other skills, they may be perceived as less tolerant of those who aren't continuously trying to improve as a know-it-all. Or they might take on too much or face burnout, the typical workaholic.

During my interviews, I found out this was how Victor's team viewed him. When this is the case, I ask a client: "How do you define work-life balance? How does your answer impact your team members who may hold a different definition?" I also posed these questions to Victor.

"Success in my field is the predictable result of following company principles and working hard, and that's what I want to model for my team," he told me. "I think I have a good work-life balance and I demonstrate that to my team."

Victor believed that before he was appointed CEO, the average team member took more responsibility for his own productivity and career success than when he started heading up the company. "I really wish that were true today," he said.

I suspected it was Victor's wish that his team members actually picked up what he perceived as slack and it was probably one of the reasons he came across as inflexible.

The Work

Over time, I helped Victor realize many things in life are the result of a "both/and" instead of an "either/or" approach. There are often different, yet valid, ways to reach the same goal. He developed the skill of curiosity, and learned to ask with genuine interest about his employees' different ways of processing things.

His team responded positively because they sensed Victor cared and truly wanted to learn from them. This positively opened the lines of communication between Victor and his team, and once that occurred, generated a new synergy. As the team tore silos down, they started functioning as a well-formed unit. Creativity soared and productivity increased.

According to Dr. Reuven Bar-On's EQ-i 2.0 model, when a person scores high in assertiveness while being unbalanced with other skills, he may be perceived as aggressive or stubborn in his beliefs, not open to other opinions or responsible for an atmosphere where others don't feel comfortable sharing their opinions. During my interviews with Victor's team, I also found out these applied to how they perceived him.

I asked Victor, "When has your assertiveness not worked to your advantage? How does your team react to it?"

Victor didn't have specific answers and was at a loss to respond. After a moment's pause though, he revealed, "There are times I feel lonely, awkward, inadequate, isolated and insecure since I've taken on this leadership position. I'm also scared."

This made sense because he had given up a job he knew so well for one in which he'd have to learn new skills. "By building your empathy skills, you'll grow into a beloved leader who'll inspire your team through positive emotional expression," I told him. By combining high assertiveness, which he already possessed, with high empathy, or warmth, Victor would be a well-rounded, impactful leader and a Star Performer CEO.

Victor had wondered what and who people were expecting as a replacement for the legendary curmudgeon who had proceeded him. "This made me nervous, so I faked it and wasn't my authentic self," he told me. "I know I had become defensive, controlling, short-tempered, bottom line-oriented and non-relational as a result of my fear."

"Don't worry," I assured him. "Increased insight has the potential to precipitate change, as long as you consistently follow through afterward. You need to reframe your thoughts and emotions to provoke sustained behavioral change." My remarks lifted his spirits, and I was certain he had the courage, as well as a strong commitment, to persevere.

To strengthen his reserve, I suggested Victor perceive himself as someone who possessed his own unique charisma. "With your wealth of knowledge and experience, you're well-qualified to encourage and inspire your direct reports," I said.

Although we focused primarily on building Victor's empathy skills, we needed to also improve his self-regard so it would be in balance with his high self-actualization score. To address this, there were times I put on my therapist's hat to help him work through the kinds of childhood wounds we all share. He had a pervasive sense of shame lingering unresolved from early childhood through adolescence, and it was holding him back.

I hypothesized that untreated irrational thoughts were blocking the natural flow of his self-regard and empathy for himself and others. We used the ABCDE exercise (it's included at the end of the book) to tease out and label these irrational thoughts one by one, until we were satisfied we'd captured the main culprits. Most of them involved typical childish explanations and rationalizations for things that befall most of us.

The irrational thought that seemed to get Victor's way most often was: "Why me? This isn't fair!" We worked with these and other victim-type thoughts and used affirmations to reframe his negative self-talk into positive self-support for mastering his goals. We softened Victor's internal critic and relaxed his high standards that other people read as exacting and idealistic. As we worked to clear out the latent residue of shame, Victor became gentler with himself.

This allowed him to become less controlling, expectant, judgmental and harsh with his team. In turn, they responded to his newfound vulnerability, which they experienced as human and genuine. It drew them closer to him, and they became more communicative with him and engaged in their work.

The Results

Experience has taught me that self-regard, emotional self-awareness and emotional expression are foundational for building the other EQ-i 2.0 skills. For Victor to step fully into his role as a resonant leader, we spent time building up these other skills. To help him develop greater emotional expression, we focused on more effective communication skills, such as learning reflective listening, modulating his tone of voice, and building his awareness of facial expressions and body postures to convey emotional support and warmth. We used real-life situations from both the office and home for our practice sessions and role-playing exercises. The work we did to identify irrational thoughts from his early childhood and then reframing them helped Victor improve both self-regard and emotional self-awareness.

I taught Victor to pay attention to the signals his body sent him. "You sometimes experience physical symptoms like neck or shoulder tension, stiffness in your joints, perspiration around your collar or a faster heartbeat," I told him. "It's important to learn what emotions these physical signs represent."

"When my heart beats faster and I get hot around the collar, that means I'm getting anxious or I want to control a situation," he told me.

Once Victor recognized that, he self-soothed and practiced slowing down, breathing deeply, and thinking more consciously. He taught himself he could trust his own instincts, as well as those of his team, and that everything usually worked out just fine. This mind shift prevented him from becoming overly involved with every project, funneling him more energy.

Victor was extremely gifted and intelligent, and often created his own homework assignments. Over time he became more patient (impulse control), adaptable and easygoing (flexibility), relaxed and personable (interpersonal relationships). Mostly, he became more comfortable in his own skin. That translated into being more genuine and conveying more empathy. As a result, his team relaxed, responding to him in a more cohesive manner.

Victor's company culture slowly changed to reflect his more personable leadership style. Because of these changes, he became more approachable as a leader and it followed naturally that team members were more apt to drop by his office and seek his advice. This new team behavior was a direct reflection of the development of Victor's empathy.

His team perceived him as being more vulnerable in what and how he shared with people and they responded in kind to his lead. Since the team felt more inspired by Victor's leadership, they started generating even more revenue.

Building Your Interpersonal Relationships

As you've learned, interpersonal relationships are key in the workplace, and to successful leadership. Business intimacy isn't a weakness; rather it's a higher-level strength when you know how to share appropriate emotional information about yourself that's relevant to the other person and the business situation. Most likely, on some level, you know what's appropriate to share: details of your divorce aren't, but concerns about a big sales presentation or shared events are.

Saying, "Wow, I'm nervous about this big client presentation," makes you appear human and vulnerable to your coworker, sending the message, "I trust you." Trust is reciprocal, so your coworkers will likely share similar emotional information with you.

When you're emotionally intimate, it means you're not hiding who you are or pretending to be someone else. You're sharing your authentic self with your coworkers and direct reports, sending them the message that you're comfortable with yourself and your abilities, rendering you even more of an effective role model and leader.

Exercises for Exploration and Mastery: Interpersonal Skills

Interpersonal relationships need to be based on a mutual give-and-take to be sustainable and satisfying over the long haul. In the old order, many relationships were based on a quid pro quo approach: "I'll scratch your back if you scratch mine." In the new paradigm, most people are starting to understand you need to give before you receive. When relationships are based on the principle of giving, both parties benefit from the co-creation of reciprocal trust, and this generates more good feelings for everyone.

By contrast, when you wait to give until after you've received, this stingy attitude conveys that you're skeptical and don't really trust the other person. This can be self-defeating and cause the other party to shrink back from the relationship. Keep in mind that it isn't appropriate to over-give, either. When I see a client has scored very high in social responsibility and low in self-regard, I wonder if he gives too much to others without taking good care of himself, which could be a sign of codependency. As with all the other EQ-i 2.0 skills in this model, finding the right balance of give-and-take is an intuitive art more than a rational science.

Knowing and determining the right degree of emotional intimacy to cultivate with a particular person is also important. I spent a year living in France and noticed a different cultural attitude than my own when making friends with Europeans who attended the same university. While I tended to dive right in and act as close friends soon after meeting someone, I noticed Europeans, while cordial and friendly, held back and got to know me before declaring me their friend.

While there's no right or wrong here, it's helpful to be mindful and attuned to other people's sensitivities. It's almost always better to take your time rather than rush to a conclusion. Because I'm a high extrovert, I always have to be mindful not to rush in too soon when forming my opinions about possible friendships.

Exercise 1

Audit your relationships for mutuality. Make a list of your relationships. You can arrange them in segments or categories as follows according to how closely you're connected to them: your primary relationship, family, very close friend, friend, business acquaintance and so on. I imagine these segments in various degrees of decreasing closeness and importance. Now look at each relationship, and write down the positives and negatives of the relationship as you see it.

Your Takeaway: Think about these questions: Can you determine whether the relationship is fulfilling or merely an obligation? How well do you know and trust the person, and how well do they know and trust you? Is your give-and-take, or back-and-forth energy, in balance or out of balance? What changes do you want to make to your relationships to help them be more balanced? Does each relationship reflect the right degree of emotional intimacy and sharing on your part, or does it need to be adjusted?

Exercise 2

Examine your boundaries. It's usually appropriate to share your deepest thoughts with your partner or primary relationship person, and it's usually not appropriate to share your private life with a business acquaintance you know from a distance. For instance, it wouldn't be appropriate to share your negative feelings about your divorce with the checker at the grocery store, but it could be appropriate to let a boss or colleague know you're having a rough day and not working at your best. That would be a demonstration of high EQ-i 2.0 because you'd convey important information that your boss or colleague might need to know.

Imagine there's a presentation that day for a high-profile client. You'd want your boss or colleague to know you need a little extra support that day to be at your best. However, you wouldn't want them to know all the gory details of your private life. Look at the relationships you noted in Exercise 1 and consider whether you behave appropriately with respect to keeping good boundaries when you're interacting with them. If not, what do you need to change about your behavior to bring things back to appropriate boundaries?

Your Takeaway: No business colleague wants to hear more than is appropriate to share, as it can cause awkwardness and embarrassment for them.

Exercise 3

Know your relationship triggers. Spend some time figuring out what type of relationship situations tend to be emotionally charged for you, and identify circumstances in which you need to stop and think before you say something or act inappropriately. Your self-regard and emotional self-awareness can help you here.

Your Takeaway: Knowing and understanding yourself well can prevent you from saying or doing something you may regret later.

Story Two: Brie

empathy: the ability to be aware of, understand and appreciate others' feelings.
social responsibility: the ability to be a cooperative, contributing and constructive member of your social group.

Empathy is the ability to put yourself in another person's shoes, see things from their point of view and understand how they'd feel or how they'd think. You don't have to agree with them; you just have to be able to stay emotionally connected to them without judgement. My training and experience has taught me people want to be seen, heard and understood. If you can understand others, they usually feel validated without the need for you to agree with their point of view. When this occurs, you've been successful in making an authentic connection with someone, and that's very valuable.

Empathy has to be in balance with assertiveness to be effective. In my personal experience of assessing clients with the EQ-i 2.0 model, most women score more than 10 points higher in empathy compared to assertiveness, while for most men, it's the opposite. Remember, any time that you score more than 10 points higher or lower than another EQ-i 2.0 skill, you're out of balance.

Empathy comes intuitively to me, being a woman and also a more sensitive person who grew up in a household of chaos and drama. Having high empathy today is definitely an asset. It helps me feel my way into what my client's issues are and understand them very quickly. Before I started working on my own EQ-i 2.0 skillset, however, my empathy was out of balance with my assertiveness.

What did this look like and how did it affect my overall ability to help my clients? It meant in my career's early days, I was overly concerned with hurting people's feelings, or creating unnecessary resistance to my suggestions and ideas. I wasn't as direct or challenging as I could have been in situations where doing so would help move the client forward. By intentionally focusing on offering my thoughts as an opinion, or even as floating a hypothesis, instead of as a declaration of truth, I made progress in being more assertive. Often, I noticed clients thanked me for being more direct and told me how valuable my opinion was to them. Today, there are still times when I express myself directly and a client is resistant or even angry with me, but this doesn't happen as often as I thought it would and we're usually able to work out any tension it causes, so the conflict is temporary.

When I was younger, I asked my father, who was a successful CFO of a well-known, privately held company, to share some of his secrets of success. One thing he told me was to never judge another person until you've walked in their shoes. This advice has always stayed with me, and I'm happy to notice all the research that has sprung up recently showing the most successful CEOs score high in empathy.

However, don't confuse empathy with sympathy, which can involve feeling pity for another person. Pity often implies we're in a better spot than the person we're "feeling sorry" for; sympathy can also imply we agree with the other person's position or that we're experiencing the same feelings. This is different than empathy, which signals we understand and care about the other person's perspective, but don't necessarily agree with it.

Hand in hand with empathy, social responsibility involves caring for and getting involved with a group larger than yourself, such as your family, church, company or community. This involvement has been proven to help reduce the risk of serious stress-induced illness. Many of my clients express this principle when they tell me having a mission or personal focus greater than themselves gives them a high degree of meaning and purpose, and motivates them to execute their goals.

However, it's important to remember that social responsibility behaviors can be underdone and overdone. Most people who want to improve their social responsibility most likely are underdoing those behaviors. If you do increase them, you'll need to ensure you don't overdo them to the point where you're ignoring your own needs. Balance is key, since you don't want to become codependent, which means you give so much to others that you ignore your own interests and needs.

Brie's Story

Brie was a bright-eyed young woman from Chapel Hill, North Carolina, where she had been a loyal Tar Heel. With black hair cut into a bob, she was a hard-working, energetic 27-year-old.

The first time we met, Brie admitted she didn't feel "good enough" about herself and really wanted to be good at what she did. Her EQ-i 2.0 report confirmed these feelings: She scored really low in self-regard. She admitted to being very hard on herself most of the time.

This was evident in her harsh negative self-talk that told her, "You should be doing more, better, and you need to get everything right." Brie felt she was the only one in her family with a high need to get everything right and this isolated her from them at times. "I want to understand why being perfect is so important to me," she told me.

Brie, who always looked professional and put-together as a CPA in public accounting, had trouble balancing her own needs and wants with those of other people, especially when it came to her family. She experienced cycles of all-or-nothing work patterns where she bounced back and forth between two extremes: In several consecutive meetings with me, she said she worked overtime in the evenings after dinner and all weekend, and didn't engage much with her family. Then, during several more consecutive meetings, she said she worked no overtime, which meant she engaged much more with her family, and daydreamed about being a stay-at-home mom.

The Evaluation

When I asked Brie to identify the biggest changes she wanted to make as a result of our work together, she said:

- I want to do a 360-degree turnaround in all aspects of my life because I feel like I could do more and I feel inadequate all around.

- I want to decrease my anxiety, which manifests as feelings of constantly forgetting something, missing something or wondering if I did something wrong.

- I want to be more giving and others-focused so I can be a better mother and wife.

- I want to understand my mother's and father's reasons for making the choices they made so we can have a better relationship.

- I want to improve my professional performance.

- I want to handle stress better.

With that in mind, these are the goals I suggested we work to:

- Increase her self-regard to help her feel less anxious about her performance

- Increase her stress tolerance to help her be more flexible and less anxious at work and home

- Draw on her high empathy score to improve her interpersonal relationships skills

- Balance her empathy with interpersonal relationships and social responsibility skills to achieve a balanced and strong Interpersonal Composite

- Increase her daily fulfillment, contentment and satisfaction with all aspects of her life to improve her overall happiness and well-being.

It was awkward to explain to Brie that most people can't make a "360-degree turnaround in all areas of life" immediately: That's too broad a goal. "It's more effective to focus on making one change at a time, step by step, so it's sustainable," I told her.

Brie was disappointed to hear this because she was an intense overachiever and driven to make changes all at once. "I'd like you to consider whether your intense emotion and constant motion might be partly responsible for your chronic sense of physical and mental exhaustion," I said.

Brie's interpersonal relationships score was low, and Dr. Reuven Bar-On's model tells us effective leadership is built upon strong relationship skills. Even if a leader has strong technical skills, she still needs to be seen as approachable and relatable to fully engage and influence people. This ability to resonate with people is known as "resonant leadership" and is examined and further explored in the book *Primal Leadership: Realizing the Power of Emotional Intelligence* by Daniel Goleman.

According to her leadership report, Brie's lower score indicated she had trouble gaining buy-in, coaching, instilling trust and garnering the resources she needed to lead her team and reach organizational goals.

She needed to build her interpersonal relationships skills to be an effective leader.

Although Brie genuinely liked the people she worked with, she hadn't made it a priority to get to know them at a deeper, more personal level and wasn't fully aware of their talents and interests. Instead, she always focused on results and production. Since she knew her coworkers at a surface level and didn't know what values they held dear or how to reach them, this inhibited her ability to motivate and inspire them. In return, they didn't know Brie well either, and this lack of rapport prevented the team from sharing valuable information with her.

In this way, Brie's ability to make well-informed decisions was limited. Brie was also quick to rely on her own devices to get the job done rather than asking for help or delegating appropriately. Her approach wasn't as efficient and her team wasn't as productive as they could be.

"It's time-consuming and frustrating to manage my team," Brie told me. "I really don't like the kind of work I'm doing or my firm's culture. There's constant pressure to perform, and I'm not good at handling stress on a daily basis." She wanted to work at another firm with a less frenetic culture. She also wanted more time with her family: "I want to leave work at work when I head home," she told me.

The Work

Being naturally proactive, Brie started a job search and landed a position at another company fairly quickly. She believed this would be a 9-to-5-style job where she wouldn't have to work nights and weekends and could have more time for her family. She told me both she and her family were excited and happy for her to begin this new position.

Brie thought this new chapter in her work life would allow her to feel more confident. After a short break from her previous job, she started her new job, but before long she felt overwhelmed again: "It seems there's always something I need to do, so I never get to do what I want to do," she told me. "When you have kids, you only get about an hour a day to do what you want."

She had feelings of inadequacy she described as "almost to the point of paranoia." Although Brie liked her new position, she still worried all the time and couldn't shake off a sense of being inadequate. I told Brie this was called imposter syndrome.

To help her counteract these negative feelings, I advised her, "Try to take an inventory of your life and identify when and where else you feel this way. Can you observe any patterns that emerge?" For example, Brie could discover that whenever she's spending too much time at work and not enough time at home or socializing with friends, she feels like she's missing out on life's best moments. I suspected whenever she made a significant life change, such as switching jobs, she felt inadequate and worked more hours to compensate for her negative thoughts regardless of whether her firm required this.

This assignment provoked a meaningful discussion, and Brie identified patterns that produced feelings of incompetence. "Your low score in reality testing is holding you back from seeing things objectively," I said. "Even though you have these feelings, they're inaccurate because in reality you're extremely competent and doing a great job."

When I asked her if she liked her new position, she said yes. "In my new job, the cultural dynamics are very different from my previous employer," Brie told me. "That culture created a constant sense of urgency and meeting deadlines, and my new firm's workload ebbs and flows, which suits me better."

However, at our next meeting, Brie reported a lack of fulfillment in what she had accomplished at her new firm to date. She constantly prepped for meetings and was a bundle of nerves before each one. I wondered about her emotional self-awareness because these comments seemed incongruent with those from our previous meeting.

"I'm working more evenings and weekends and checking my phone for messages more frequently in my off-time," she told me. "I feel like I'm not doing enough at work."

Brie's anxiety also took a toll on her body. At night, she ruminated about all the things she wasn't getting done, so she couldn't fall asleep easily, and when she did, she didn't stay asleep. In the morning, she didn't wake up refreshed.

As so often happens in my coaching work, I discovered issues from Brie's family life intertwined with her business life. We spent the next few months discussing her concerns about balancing time between work and family with her fears she was an inadequate mother and wife.

During one of our discussions, I asked her to walk me through a typical workday. I discovered she usually worked 10-hour days with no breaks, even for lunch. Then she went home for dinner with her family, put the kids to bed and went back to her laptop to do more work before turning in at midnight. In addition, she often worked over the weekend, as she did with her previous job. I saw this as a continuation of a pattern and expressed my concerns to her. I put on my marriage and family therapist hat and suggested that spousal and family relationships thrive with lots of attention and suffer when the opposite occurs.

With the additional stress of emotionally caretaking for her mother, who was in an extended inpatient physical therapy program, Brie's work pattern wasn't sustainable. Over time, she reported having headaches and migraines, and was dismayed to see she had become more irritable with her family. This information helped me realize her lack of interpersonal relationship skills stemmed from her lack of self-regard and poor stress management skills, and we needed to address this at every meeting.

Brie fueled her inner turmoil by constantly second-guessing herself, wondering if she was doing everything right, and thinking of all the things she wasn't getting done. This inner battle cost her a lot of energy and drained her so much that she snapped at her family members, those with whom she felt most comfortable expressing herself.

I insisted she increase her self-care and take the time to stick to an exercise schedule of three to four times per week. She made honest attempts and continued to struggle with time for these activities.

A lot of my female clients who are high achievers, or perfectionists, come from a background where they were forced to grow up fast and take on adult responsibilities too soon. The carefree part of their childhoods was terminated and they became mini-adults with a serious nature practically overnight. In some cases, this was because they had to step in and help the family because of an illness, accident or tragedy. In others, it was due to mental illness or the deficiency of the adults' parenting skills. When Brie said she felt like the rug was going to get pulled out from her feet at any moment, she clued me in to the possibility that she belonged to this troubled tribe of trauma survivors.

I asked if we could explore her family background, including her growing-up years. This proved to be valuable when my suspicions were confirmed. As Brie recounted significant events in her adult life, I discovered several incidents that were a cause of severe shame. In fact, her shame was so great she hadn't forgiven herself. I suggested it was crucial she create and execute rituals to help her let go of the shame and accept she did the best she could at the time.

"One of the best ways you can do this is to ask yourself what you learned from this experience, and how it made you a stronger, more resilient person," I told Brie. "I'd like you to reflect on whether you'd make the same choices again. If you knew then what you know now, would you do it the same way? Write about this every day in your journal, so you can work toward forgiving and accepting yourself."

As she worked on this assignment, some chaotic and conflictual events happened in Brie's family life. She was so upset that significant fight-or-flight feelings were triggered by some family members' behavior. Brie was experiencing these feelings partly because she didn't feel heard by her family. "I want to be a priority with them," she told me, and I wondered if they felt she didn't make them a priority, so they were all caught in a catch-22 cycle of ignoring behavior.

"You need to make forgiving yourself a priority before your family will follow suit," I told her.

If Brie wanted to improve her relationships with others, she needed to solidify her relationship with herself first. This included taking care of herself and making sure she lived consistently with her most important values. For example, she wasn't taking her own emotional or physical needs seriously, and then expected her family to compensate for what she wouldn't do for herself. In response, she felt her family ignored her needs and she lived on the brink of depression.

One of the ways I helped motivate Brie was to appeal to her desire to become more emotionally intelligent than any of her parents or grandparents. She told me neither of her parents had good relationships with their parents, and the same was true for both sets of grandparents. Her father was physically abusive to his wife and children, and her mother was unstable and couldn't hold down a steady job.

The atmosphere Brie grew up in was chaotic and dramatic, and she adapted by becoming very organized and responsible. Since she was good at problem-solving, Brie was already more emotionally intelligent than her parents, but she needed to improve her self-regard, as well as Interpersonal Composite skills to truly transcend the family legacy.

The Results

At this point in our work together, Brie said lowering her anxiety while building confidence and trust in her own abilities was her most important goal. One of the ways she tried to overcome her insecurities was to take continuing education classes. Although this was a positive compensation behavior, I suggested she start noting her many accomplishments on a daily basis. "Catch yourself doing things 'right' or 'well,' and write them down in your journal," I told her.

"I'm focusing on where I can provide the most value instead of spreading myself too thin," she said.

"That's definitely a step in the right direction and will help you feel less scattered and more organized," I replied.

My hypothesis proved true over time. By taking on less and focusing on areas of her life where she could have the greatest impact, Brie increased her belief in her own abilities. She felt less like she was randomly skating her way through life and more like she was empowered by a sense of meaning and purpose. This purpose included learning to be more patient with her family and intentionally reaching out to connect with dear friends on a more regular basis. She learned to ask for help from family, friends and her staff more often, giving her a feeling of connection and support with other people that helped her increase her stress tolerance and sense of well-being. She didn't feel as isolated or alone with her own problems anymore.

Although Brie continues to actively work on feeling confident at work, her improved relationship skills are evident in the increased engagement she has with her coworkers and her team. Overall there's a new sense of rhythm and flow in her department, so productivity has increased and projects are better organized.

Building Your Empathy and Social Responsibility

When you consider your own empathy, try this: Impartially observe yourself while conversing with others. When someone talks to you, are you really listening to her, or are you already internally prepping your own response? Many people already leap to their own response; it's a common, non-empathetic habit, but it impairs communication. If you realize you're engaging in this very normal habit, there are some steps you can take to guide yourself toward being more empathetic.

First, when you notice that your mind is leaping ahead, nudge yourself back to consciously hear what the other person is saying to you. It's not necessary for you to agree with the other person, so you can give yourself permission to just hear their point of view. You also don't need to attach your values, feelings, thoughts or opinions to the other person's statements. Don't feel you must cross any bridge to agree with her; you can see things differently, and that's OK.

Social responsibility is a healthy way to connect to the larger world, whether it's your family and friends, church, company, your community or a cause you're passionate about. It also encompasses acting in a socially responsible manner, even though it may not benefit you personally, so you behave in an ethical manner and honor societal rules and social norms. You have a social consciousness and the willingness to do something for your team, department, organization, or for society, with no direct benefit to yourself.

EQ-i 2.0 incorporates morality and consciousness. While a person is born with an intrinsic IQ, you have to work to grow your emotional intelligence skills. A leader with a high IQ but little sense of social responsibility may tend to be self-absorbed and inner focused, while a leader with high social responsibility will turn his attention outward to meet the community's greater good while still accomplishing his corporate goals.

Helping others often ends up helping yourself indirectly. I often hear stories of clients who've donated large amounts of their time helping on nonprofit boards, who found their efforts got them noticed by people with large spheres of influence. Sometimes their donated time led to making influential connections with people who offered them a better job, a new client, recognition and awards, or a speaking engagement.

By contrast, I've had clients who couldn't say "no" to helping others, often at the expense of themselves or getting their own jobs done and their employer's needs met. On occasion, these clients were addicted to the kind of high they experienced when they felt needed. This type of social responsibility is overdone, because it's seductive and dependent on a constant need to be needed, which is a type of dependency. If you see yourself in this example, circle back to working on your self-regard, so you can meet your need to be needed intrinsically before volunteering any more time and effort for others' benefit.

Once you feel confident you can generate good feelings about yourself on your own, then go back to helping others with a clearer perspective. That way, you'll be more independent and effective. There's an unhealthy risk in caring too much for others' concerns, even if your concern is for your own company. Burnout from overdoing takes a long time to recover from emotionally, spiritually and physically.

Exercises for Exploration and Mastery: Empathy and Social Responsibility

Now, work on the exercises that resonate most with you.

Exercise 1

See things from another person's point of view. Think of a person who has a viewpoint different than your own, maybe someone with whom conversing with is difficult. Reflect on how you could put yourself in their shoes and see things from their point of view, and attempt to understand it. What kinds of experiences did they have that might be different from yours that led to the formation of how they see the world? What else might be true about them or their background that you don't know?

Your Takeaway: Given this person's truth or background, does it make sense how they see the world the way they do? How does that change your perspective about interacting with someone who has a different viewpoint?

Exercise 2

Take it even further. For a real challenge, invite a conversation with this person, or someone else whose viewpoint you have trouble understanding without reacting emotionally. Practice giving them your full attention while listening to what they have to say. Be still, and really listen as if you're trying to memorize their words. Notice how you feel. Are you squirming in your seat as you listen? Are you sweaty, have a knot in your stomach or tension in your shoulders? Do you fight your need to respond emotionally or keep silent? Practice detaching from your emotional responses. Repeat back to them what you heard them say. Tell them you understand their point of view.

Your Takeaway: Remember, you can offer understanding to another person without offering agreement or adopting it yourself.

Exercise 3

Find a cause you care about and find a volunteer opportunity. If you don't have the experience of being on a committee or a board for a cause you care about, create that for yourself. It's a very rewarding and valuable experience to sit on a committee or nonprofit board, pitch in, and help make things happen. Reflect on your experience.

Your Takeaway: How has volunteering changed your perspective on your life, and your role in the larger world?

Exercise 4

If you're an over-giver, review your volunteer activities. Make a list of every professional group or organization you volunteer for and discern where you're giving too much of your time and care. Where can you pare down or cut back?

Your Takeaway: Decide, and then resign from those things that steal your energy without giving you a sense of meaning and purpose.

Exercise 5

Review your roles. Consider the different roles you play: spouse, mother or father, sister or brother, son or daughter, grandchild, friend, or business acquaintance. Consider how good a job you do in this role, how much time you spend on it and how empathically supportive you are to the people who depend on you. What grade would you give yourself in each of your roles? Which need improvement? What do you need to do to be better in that role?

Your Takeaway: Review, decide and then resign from those things that steal your energy without giving you a sense of meaning and purpose.

Exercise 6

Consider another person's feelings before speaking. When you're about to give a directive to a direct report, your staff or even your life partner, take a moment to consider how they'll hear and interpret your message and how they'll feel about it. Put yourself in their shoes.

Your Takeaway: Think about how you'd feel if the roles were reversed.

Exercise 7

Break out of your self-absorption. Take time to ask someone else how their day is going, and truly care to hear the answer. Listen well, and offer some sincere and positive feedback.

Your Takeaway: How did it feel to reach out to someone else and give them unselfish, genuine attention and affirmation?

Part IV

Decision-Making Composite

Story One: Emily

problem solving: the ability to identify and define
problems as well as to generate and implement
potentially effective solutions.

All of us have problems: It's the human condition. Plus, since we have
to make a living, our time in the workplace involves solving a series of
problems every day. The better your problem-solving skills, the more
successful you'll be.

Let's imagine your boss calls a quick meeting with you on a Friday
at 4 p.m. and says tersely, "Your sales team isn't hitting their quotas this
month. You need to get them back on track!" This scenario is far from
unusual across most job roles in most industries because there's always
a problem that needs to be solved.

If your problem-solving skills are low, you might react to this type
of meeting with destructive self-talk like, "I can't stand to deal with this
kind of problem," "I'll never get this right," "If I screw this up, I might
get fired," or "Any failure means that I'm a failure!" That self-talk would
likely lower your self-confidence that you could get your team's numbers back up, and you may freeze up altogether and not be able to function in solving the problem at all.

On the other hand, if you consider what you've done previously
when your sales team's numbers were lower than expected, you can create a proven problem-solving plan.

This could include items like reviewing the month's numbers against
the prior month and year-over-year; meeting with your sales reps to
learn what's happening in the field and what help they might need; or
talking with your marketing department to see what messaging they

could get out to prospects and customers. In this way, you can develop a strategy to solve the problem, plus you engender renewed confidence in your boss and team.

People who are the most successful problem solvers usually have the following characteristics:

- They have a systemic approach they replicate, whether conscious or unconscious, to facing a problem and considering solutions.

- They don't let their emotions cloud their thinking, meaning they can stay objective and see the bigger picture.

- They're good at using their intuition, creativity or gut feelings to find solutions, and they can accurately assess both the risks and the benefits to trying an out-of-the-box approach.

Be aware that the majority of problems you face at work will require you to use both your emotional intelligence and your IQ to find the best solution.

A very basic and important emotional intelligence tenet is the ability to govern and regulate your emotions so they don't run your life. This ability is an important factor when you're problem-solving, because it's usually not in your best interests to attempt to solve a problem when your emotions have hijacked you – and you have little control over them.

As a point of reference, this tenet ties into Daniel Goleman's concept of emotional hijacking and the reptile brain, also known as the amygdala, which protected us from death by saber-toothed tigers back in cavepeople days. Also known as the fight-or-flight syndrome, it triggered an adrenaline-cortisol response to keep us alive in the presence of real and imminent danger. In short, it played an important role as a basic survival mechanism.

While there are no saber-toothed tigers confronting humans today, this part of our brain still functions to keep us safe, albeit in a primitive, awkward way. When deep emotions get triggered in the form of irrational thoughts embedded in the unconscious coming up for air, they can induce a fight-or-flight state in us, even though there's no immediate physical threat. The effects on the human body are the same though, and often we unconsciously rush ahead without the guiding principle of conscious, rational thought and do or say something self-destructive we later regret. In these moments, we truly lack control over our impulses because our reptile brain sacrifices speed for accuracy and isn't very emotionally intelligent.

When I think of a lack of problem solving and impulse control, I think of one pretty, bright, talented and gifted client in particular. When Emily first came to see me, she was having trouble finishing her master's degree at night while working full-time during the day. She'd been attending school for five years, but hadn't completed her degree. She was only halfway through the credits required to graduate, and many of the classmates she started with had already graduated and scored jobs in their chosen fields, so she felt left behind. While she had good intentions of finishing up the coursework for her degree, she allowed other dramatic events in her life related to family and friends to consistently pull her off course.

Emily lived in the moment, capriciously living day to day without a sense of plot-tying her days together: She had no long-term strategic plan, and she couldn't decide who she wanted to be. Although she was studying finance and accounting in her fifth year of her master's degree, she switched majors again to economics and didn't know when or how she'd qualify for graduation. If her original agenda had been to complete her degree as soon as possible, she was nowhere near completion now because she kept changing her mind. She couldn't commit herself fully to any one particular field of study, and had trouble narrowing down her list of choices. Because of her inability to make up her mind, she was like an eternal girl always drifting, and she was dependent on an academic structure to give her a sense of meaning and purpose.

Emily's main problem was that she had no end-game. She hadn't taken the time to reflect on her values or skills, in an attempt to figure out how she could best use them to make a difference in the world. In addition, she had little idea of what type of work would bring her emotional fulfillment and career success. As a result, she changed her mind repeatedly as she tried out different options. Even when starting her new semester of classes, for example, she'd already lamented she had chosen incorrectly. She had a myriad of excuses: She didn't like the instructors, the assigned projects were uninteresting, and her classmates were underdeveloped and boring. Because of her lack of conviction in her own decisions, she often showed up late or missed her classes altogether. She often asked professors for extensions on assignments, and I got the feeling they were frustrated with her, wanting to pass her on to the next instructor.

Because Emily's family life with her parents, brothers and sisters was chaotic and unfocused, they had a negative effect on her career progress. Her undue concern for her family's approval of her choices and the way she conducted her life also distracted her from performing her best when she was at her sales-focused day job: By the time she arrived at her desk, she was emotionally drained from the night before. She wasn't skilled at maintaining a work-life balance, either, because her family and social life garnered most of her attention. She feared that sooner or later her ability to perform at the top of her peer group would decline. She wondered if her boss noticed when she slacked off, and she felt guilty putting her family and social priorities in front of her tasks during the workday.

Emily's Story

Emily was an M.B.A. student from Washington University, with long curly hair and a heart-shaped face. Petite at 5'2", she was athletic and loved bicycling the Katy Trail on long weekends with friends.

Emily was cheerful, pleasant and professional when she first came to consult with me. She strode into my office with a smile, her bright energy filling the room that sunny day. It didn't take long for me to realize Emily's seemingly positive demeanor was a well-rehearsed mask, artfully cultivated to pass for charm in the sales world.

She came prepared, and handed me a list of goals she wanted to address: to establish more self-confidence; to feel more fulfilled in her career; to learn to manage her impulses and spend less time on empty, meaningless socializing; to change her negative mindset to positive; and to have a better work-life balance.

Emily was immediately open with me and shared the following: "What I want most is to gain confidence so I can pursue my dreams and become all I want to be," she said. This sounded very much like self-actualization, and I was excited to hear her say this because it suggested she was coachable.

Emily also said she was a quarter of the way through her life and didn't like the person she was or the direction she was headed. "I don't want the way I'm living to become my way of life in the future," she told me. "The very thought of living this way forever scares me, and makes my heart beat fast and my stomach ache."

In addition to these goals, she wanted to finish school and secure a better job. She asked for my help in determining a career direction that suited her personality. The way she phrased her desire was interesting. She said she didn't want to do something anymore just because it looked good on paper or because she thought she'd be admired for it. "I want to do something I'm passionate about so I'll be excited to wake up in the morning and go to work," she told me. "I don't feel that way now at all."

At the end of our initial meeting, Emily added that she wasn't good at managing her finances and wanted assistance with making better financial decisions. She indicated her money situation was askew, not because she didn't know how to manage her money, but because she couldn't keep her emotional impulses from sabotaging her budget plans.

The Evaluation

One of the critical things I often ask clients is: Was there a time when your life was different, better or more like how you wanted it to be? This questioning technique is called "searching for the exception" to your general perception. I usually ask this because if a person has been able to do something once, she's created a template in her brain that allows for the possibility of being able to do the same thing again.

Often, the client has falsely convinced herself there's never been an exception to her present circumstances. When we search for and find the memory of it, our restorative work has begun. When I asked Emily to find the exception, she cried and agreed the situation in which she now found herself hadn't always been true. "I want to find my way back to how I used to be," she said. This didn't seem as daunting to her as finding her way to becoming an entirely new person.

"I used to be at the top of my class in high school," Emily told me. In fact, she was president of the student council, volunteered at her church and tutored elementary students on the side. She remembered that during this time of her life she felt spiritually connected and excited about her future. Emily was confident in her abilities and had a sense of inner security; she felt good about herself and didn't need to turn to others, such as a boyfriend, for self-affirmation. In addition, she managed her money well. And by the time she graduated high school, Emily was senior class valedictorian.

When I asked Emily what had happened between that point and when we started working together, she was thoughtful and answered truthfully that her heart had been broken by a boy during her college years. As a freshman in college, Emily met another student named Adam and quickly fell in love. They dated on and off until Emily graduated with her bachelor's degree. Their relationship was dramatic and rocky, and when Emily worried about it, she shut down and didn't study, do her homework or relate to anyone else. Her grades fell, and unlike at her high school graduation, Emily was far from being class valedictorian. In fact, she barely finished college with an average GPA.

During the early years of Emily's relationship with Adam, her family liked him and was supportive of their dating. By the end of it, however, her parents had grown weary of hearing about the up-and-down relationship and no longer approved of him. They didn't like the casual way he treated their daughter or their relationship.

At the same time, her family noticed Emily had become very needy and less independent. She was extremely close to her parents, brother, grandparents, aunts and cousins, but yearned for their acceptance and approval. Her parents were concerned, although they didn't know how to help her regain her former self-confidence and sense of initiative.

They were frustrated, and unfortunately, they chose a communication method that only made things worse with their daughter. They'd draw close to her by telephoning her too often and telling her what to do. Then they'd withdraw and stop calling, frustrated because she didn't take their advice. They didn't realize they were recreating the toxic dance that Emily and Adam were engaged in: push me, pull me, back and forth, a come-close-and-then-withdraw game. This type of communication wasn't productive and created a lot of psychic tension between Emily and her parents.

In addition, Emily's parents didn't get along well. They often disagreed with each other about how to parent their children and gave mixed signals to Emily, who worried whether their most recent argument would be their last and trigger a divorce. Without a model for what a good, healthy relationship looked like, Emily was left to conjure up her own imaginings.

Unfortunately, she was more of an idealist than a realist, and she fell in love with someone who wasn't skilled at making her feel safe, loved and secure. Emily also discovered Adam had repeatedly cheated on her, and that was the ultimate undoing of their relationship.

After this event, Emily had trouble regulating and controlling her emotional impulses. She felt untethered and lost, no longer knowing what she wanted to do with her life. To escape and avoid the pain of not knowing, she started hanging out with a wild crowd who went out and socialized every night. She binge ate without really knowing why she did it.

Emily alternated days of loading up on carbohydrates like macaroni and cheese with days of drinking nothing but water. Before long, she was in a vicious cycle she couldn't stop. She gained a lot of weight and disliked her appearance. She was still able to present herself as beautiful and professional, and I often commented on this in an attempt to boost her self-image. I referred her to an agency that could offer eating-disorder help so we could focus on building her emotional intelligence skills.

The Work

During our meetings, we slowly added new goals to Emily's original ones: to become inner-directed, less impulsive and more patient; to feel good about being alone and female; to learn to comfort herself without relying on something or someone else; and to be herself and different from her family. We had discussions and did exercises addressing all of these goals.

I talked with Emily about ways to stay in the here and now without projecting her thoughts into the past or the future. She suffered from extreme anxiety, an amount beyond what's considered normal, and this anxiety interfered with her ability to make good decisions. For example, when Emily didn't know what to do, she catastrophized her current situation. She thought about all the negative times in her past that made her feel like the current situation did, and she froze and felt like a victim. She thought she had no power or choice over the fantasized outcome, one which was always the worst one she could imagine.

Her optimism was also low, so she never thought about the opposite possibility: that everything could turn out better than she thought it would, or at least, not as bad as her negative self-talk led her to believe. Since her anxiety often overwhelmed her, I taught Emily to stop and take three deep breaths whenever she was in a situation where her anxiety caused her to be out of control. I also asked her to think about her feet firmly planted on the ground, as if they had roots like trees that connected her to the earth, making her feel tethered. "I really like this exercise because it makes me stop and take stock of my situation in a more appropriate way, instead of allowing my feelings to run me," she told me. I also emphasized daily goal-setting and assigning priorities.

Since it was a pattern for Emily to keep changing her mind about things, or to not know which daily tasks took priority over things she could put off until later, I asked her to get a Franklin Covey Planner and some colored pens. Since Emily was creative and artistic, she approached this assignment with enthusiasm. I taught her to plan her next week on Sunday afternoons. I asked her to see what school assignments were due and when, and to note that on the calendar, and the same for sales proposals at work.

Then we worked backward, Swiss-cheesing her weekly tasks, and breaking them down into bite-sized chunks that she could complete without feeling overwhelmed. Each night before bed, she reviewed her planner to assess the day's progress and made revisions for the next day based on that outcome. Done on a daily basis, this exercise helped Emily gain control over her decisions. This exercise became a valued habit for her, and as she continued to use it, she began to feel a sense of empowerment about her ability to work independently and make appropriate choices to motivate herself and govern her behavior.

Emily also used her planner to make a budget and track her daily, weekly and monthly expenses. The same exercise that helped her track her school and work assignments also gave her better command over making and tracking her financial choices. To help her have greater work integrity, I asked her to set two alarms so she could wake up for work and arrive on time. Likewise for school, we established the rule of attending every class and arriving on time. To help Emily get more sleep so she could wake up refreshed for work and school, we set limits and established boundaries regarding how much time Emily spent socializing with her family and friends the night before.

Then, to build her independence and diminish her need for approval from family and friends, I asked Emily to journal her feelings, and write out justifications and pro and con lists for every major decision she made. I asked her to read these until she could stand up for every decision she made no matter what anyone else thought of it. Through my relationship with her, I modeled the dynamics of good communication and relationship skills. We made excellent progress and over time, and Emily started to feel more self-reliant.

Emily explained that after her college graduation, she was lucky to land her current job, even though it wasn't what she really wanted. Remarkably, she was one of the top salespeople in her company because she was extroverted and good at connecting with people, albeit on a surface level. Because of her well-developed interpersonal skills, she engaged potential customers and quickly closed sales. Because someone else set up Emily's appointments and did her paperwork, she was successful, despite her lack of patience and organizational skills.

In the long run, Emily was dissatisfied about her ability to advance in the boutique retail setting, which was family-owned and had its limitations in a rural town. She wanted to move to a larger city, where there would be more opportunities. Through her network of social connections, she learned about an opportunity for possible advancement at another employer, along with a strong recommendation from her friend.

Her prospective employer requested Emily send her resume and application immediately, because he wanted to fill the job opening as soon as possible. Emily was excited and asked for my help. Yet, in the face of this new possibility, Emily struggled with extreme anxiety and felt overwhelmed, which was exacerbated by further binge eating and late nights socializing.

In addition to lacking impulse control, Emily had low self-regard and stress tolerance skills. When she couldn't tolerate her anxiety and overwhelm anymore and she felt emotionally hijacked, her reptile brain triggered her to engage in escape behaviors. This is what she did instead of finishing her job application on a timely basis. Due to lack of assertiveness and fear of rejection, Emily dragged her feet for several weeks and didn't follow through, despite my promptings.

Meanwhile, we worked together on her resume. I helped Emily remember and list her accomplishments, training and credentials that would certainly make her stand out among the other sales applicants. We reviewed her educational qualifications and brainstormed appropriate personal references who could attest to her interpersonal proficiency with potential customers. Because she had high social responsibility skills, Emily cared about how her potential resignation would affect her current boss, leaving her in a jam without enough salespeople. We talked through how she could approach her supervisor and even help her find a replacement salesperson. We did everything we could to build momentum to help Emily move forward and execute her plans.

The Results

Just as we became close to succeeding, a longstanding toxic relationship with a male friend pulled Emily into an emotionally destructive soup. Emily allowed herself to become swallowed up in the drama and couldn't concentrate on executing her employment change. By the time she climbed out of her emotional prison, the job opportunity wasn't available anymore.

I included Emily's story to show that not all client stories are success stories. For every one person who succeeds, perhaps another doesn't. This doesn't mean that Dr. Reuven Bar-On's EQ-i 2.0 model we use doesn't work. The outcome to this story has everything to do with the client's particular personality, unconscious early childhood programming, and family circumstances. Sadly, this client had a family at odds with her.

Emily's complicated family structure and dynamics hindered her desire to increase her self-regard. Why? Unconsciously, she worried if she did become more independent, self-reliant and confident, and started solving her own problems, she'd lose her family's support, though it was problematic, because she feared being alone outside the family circle.

For future growth, Emily would need to focus on her lack of problem-solving skills. Early childhood programming causes all of us to make decisions with a child's mind that become embedded in our unconscious and blossom into irrational thoughts by the time we're adults. These early decisions become entrenched in fixed habit patterns, and when we become adults it's difficult, though not impossible, to alter or transform them. To do so takes an iron will, and the passion to push past your comfort zone at all costs for the prize that waits in your transformation.

Because Emily couldn't decide whether or not she was willing to undergo temporary discomfort for the possibility of delayed gratification and success, she stopped short in her development goals. When it came to taking the plunge to be her own person, regardless of what her family and friends thought, she couldn't commit to give it a go. She was too reliant on their acceptance and conversational support, even though it was often tangential to her desired outcomes and took her off track. She remained addicted to the high she felt when people close to her told her what to do so she wouldn't have to decide things for herself, even though others didn't make beneficial decisions on her behalf.

For Emily to succeed, there may need to be a time when things get so bad she desperately yearns for independence, self-regard and stress tolerance more than she wants her family's interfering presence in her life. At that point she'll need to face what she's turned her back on: the same triggers that emotionally hijack her when she's anxious. She'll need to stop using food, socializing and relationships to escape from life as it is in the moment. She must want to stand firmly on her own two feet and embrace the sparkling personality she has (that her family doesn't tolerate) and accept it as her birthright and lifetime gift. These changes would give her sufficient self-regard to build the other skills. Only then can she increase her emotional intelligence score and achieve true success and well-being.

Building Your Problem Solving

One thing that interfered with Emily's ability to problem solve was her over-the-top anxiety. While her anxiety pushed her into an extreme state of paralysis by analysis, we all have some amount of anxiety as humans. Since one antidote to anxiety is to collect more information in an attempt to alleviate it, one step in problem solving is to gather the appropriate amount of research and information before making a decision.

What if it's possible to systematize your process for weighing information and making a decision? If you develop a tried-and-true process that works for you under most circumstances, you can save yourself a lot of time and anxiety. Here's an example of how you might develop such a system:

- **Recognize that a problem exists and define it**. Be conscious and aware that this problem exists. Now, truly look at the problem and examine it from all aspects and angles. Take pen to paper, and attempt to use the most accurate words to describe the problem. Perhaps write it as a narrative and tell a story if that's possible.

- **Examine alternative points of view, imagining someone else is examining the same problem (like your direct reports, your coworkers or your boss)**. How would they describe the problem? Would they articulate it the same way you did? Would they have a different point of view? If so, write these down.

- **Gather the necessary information**. Do more research and gather as much information as you can about the problem. Interview and ask questions to any stakeholders or people involved in the implementation and resultant outcome of the solution.

- **Generate alternate solutions**. Brainstorm a list of possible solutions and write them down.

- **Evaluate the alternatives**. Make a list of pros and cons that arise in each solution, as well as a list of possible consequences and risks, both positive and negative.

- **Choose the best alternative**. Now using your best judgement, choose the best solution.

- **Incubate and verify your choice**. Sleep on your decision and watch for any feelings you have since making your decision. Re-evaluate how you feel about your choice first thing when you wake up in the morning. Make any changes that may be necessary.

- **Write out your justification**. Be aware it may not be the perfect solution, because perfection isn't possible. Write out your justification about why you chose this solution so you can stand your ground on this decision and know why you made it.

- **Act on your decision and implement it**. Know that you made the best decision you could with the information available at the time.

- **Review and evaluate the outcome**. Learn from the consequences of the decision you made. Would you do something different after knowing the outcome? If so, write it down so you can learn from it and use it for next time.

Repeating this process will help you become more confident in your decision-making ability.

I had to make a very important decision one Christmas. My husband and I were driving cross-country during a snowstorm, hoping to make it to my family's home for the holidays to see my aged father. At the time, my father was in poor health, and I was intuitively convinced he might be dying. The interstates were icy, it was snowing intensely, and we could barely see the road ahead of us. Traffic was backed up for miles. We didn't feel it was safe to keep driving, and we stopped in beautiful Louisville, Kentucky, for the evening. It was Christmas Eve, and I was terribly disappointed to still be so far from my family's home in a Chicago suburb.

The good news was that we were able to spend two nights in a beautiful, historic boutique hotel that was cozy and warm. We had a wonderful Christmas Eve dinner in the Oak Room, a once-in-a-lifetime experience. The tedious news was the forecast: no letup in sight for the next few days in the snow. Part of me wanted to forge ahead to Chicago anyway and see my father, and part of me wanted to turn around and head back to Asheville, North Carolina, where there was no snow and the roads were clear.

Though it sounds somewhat silly today, as I struggled that cold, snowy evening in the cozy, warm, beautifully decorated lobby of the old Seelbach Hotel, I was anxious about my decision. It felt like a life-and-death, heavy decision. I only made progress when I used a tried-and-true remedy: I made a handwritten list of pros and cons for each decision I could possibly make and because I did that, more information became available through my unconscious. We already knew the current weather report, but no one knew my father's true longevity. Through this process I weighed my options, and we chose to stay the evening and leave as early as possible the next morning, just in case my father really was close to death.

As things turned out, we had a short window of opportunity and were able to break through the weather early that next day. I made it home for the holidays and was able to see my father one last time, and said a very meaningful goodbye. He died 13 days later, and I've never regretted my decision to make a run for it and brave the storm. I don't believe I would have arrived at the same conclusion if I hadn't made my list, because I was poised to turn around and head back to my own home before I put pen to paper that snowy evening.

Exercises for Exploration and Mastery: Problem Solving

Successful problem solving is usually the result of combining both your intuition in the form of hunches and impressions and your creativity, or your capacity to think outside of the box and come up with a fresh perspective. There's a third component: your use of logic and sound reasoning, because innovation doesn't come without risk. You need to be able to evaluate the consequences of the risks you're are taking with a cool, impartial mindset.

Exercise 1

Overcome your anxiety when problem solving. For some people, anxiety can be a part of the problem-solving process because they're trying to find the perfect solution, or they fear failure and its consequences. Here's a common cognitive behavioral exercise for calming the mind and increasing confidence in finding the best solution. Imagine the worst-case scenario that could occur as a result of the solution you chose to a problem you're solving. Write it down and describe it in as full detail as possible.

Now ask yourself if this worst-case scenario really happens, can you survive it and tolerate the results? Can you find a way to cope with it and get through it? Now ask yourself what the best-case scenario might be. Write it down. If the best-case scenario occurs, can you deal with that? What will change in your life as a result? Now ask yourself what's most likely to happen, which is probably in the middle of the worst- and best-case results. Can you live with that outcome? What will occur as a result?

Your Takeaway: Now that your alternate cases are so well-thought-out, you'll feel much more sure of yourself and your decision-making authority.

Exercise 2

Take a break and enact your unconscious mind. Sometimes, when I try too hard to solve a problem with only logic, my brain gets locked up and I can't find the solution. Often, the kind of problem-solving I'm doing has to do with client situations and how to help them. When I lived in Flat Rock, North Carolina, I had access to the national park at Carl Sandburg's house. Every morning, I used to problem solve by hiking up Little or Big Glassy mountain. The hypnotic effect of being out in the woods, looking at the birds and the squirrels, and the rhythm of hiking used to activate my unconscious mind. Often, by the time I finished my hike, I had found my solution.

Now that I live in St. Louis, I walk mornings in my neighborhood and the magic of rhythmic walking works just the same. The unconscious mind is activated by anything that's repetitive and mundane: showering, doing dishes, vacuuming, sweeping, walking or driving. All can be helpful times to problem solve. What are your ways of taking a break and finding the solution from your unconscious mind?

Your Takeaway: Experiment to see what methods work best for you and write them down so you don't forget.

Exercise 3

Learn from the past. Make a list of major problems you've faced in your life, and write down how you solved them and how things turned out. What did you learn from the process you used? What didn't work and had to be refined?

Learn from the present. Make a list of major problems you have right now. Write down the reasons they aren't resolved. Are there any you're avoiding? If so, what's causing you to not face them? What would help you get started? What would the benefits be of having them resolved? What are the consequences of avoiding them?

Your Takeaway: Prioritize your list and decide which ones you'll tackle first. Follow the problem-solving process noted in this chapter and use it to see how things turn out.

Exercise 4

Learn from others. Think of authority figures when you were little: your parents, any older siblings, teachers or pastors. Write down how they taught you to problem solve. Now evaluate what they taught you from an adult perspective: Was their process effective or not? What methodology did you learn from them? Do you want to continue to use it? Or, is there someone in your current life who'd serve as a better role model when it comes to problem solving? If so, how can you learn or adopt their method?

Your Takeaway: Consider how crowdsourcing ways to problem solve changes your perspective on the process of looking for new solutions.

Exercise 5

Discuss problems with someone you trust. Often, I problem solve out loud with my husband, as it always helps to get his perspective. Personality-wise, on the Myers-Briggs Personality Indicator, he's the opposite of me in the indicator for how you conduct your life. I'm a "J," which means I'm methodical and detail-oriented, while he's a "P," which means he's spontaneous and can see the big picture better than I can. I often find that the combination of both our minds elicits a more holistic outcome because sometimes, without his perspective, I'm prone to get mired in the details and miss the overall best picture. Who's your sounding board? It's often true that the synergy of two heads are better than one.

Your Takeaway: Small decisions are easier to make the big decisions. Is there a way to break up your major decisions into a series of smaller steps?

Story Two: Frank

reality testing: the ability to assess the correspondence between what you experience and what objectively exists.
impulse control: the ability to resist or delay an impulse, drive, or temptation to act.

We're prone to develop preconceived ideas about situations based upon our emotions. Reality testing involves taking steps to see past our emotional hopes, fears and biases so we can recognize situations for what they really are.

Researcher Melanie Klein was an Austrian-British psychoanalyst recognized in the field of child psychology for developing and conceiving novel therapeutic techniques. As a leading innovator in object relations theory, she discovered that many of our adult thought patterns and behaviors are influenced by the way our caretakers related to us. This includes behaviors like the way they physically held us or looked at us and made eye contact, especially in the first 18 months of our lives.

Caretakers who were anxious parents tend to raise children who have anxious attachment, while parents who felt confident in their roles tend to raise children who have safe and secure attachment. By the time we reach age 23, our reactions to these early caretakers' behaviors color our perspectives on life. We tend to filter our emotions through lenses prejudiced by our own experiences, and apply those biases to others as we look outside ourselves to judge their reality. In this way, we aren't accurately assessing reality.

Reality testing involves taking steps to free ourselves from our emotionally influenced points of view, generated from our own experiences, and remove our unconscious biases so we can size up our circumstances accurately. It's also the ability to tune in and correctly assess the correspondence between what we experience and what actually exists. It's our capacity to see things as they genuinely are, not as we fear them or wish them to be.

This ability involves our skill to research or gather relevant details and information, generate alternative solutions and identify the best one: the one that will result in the most positive outcome with the least amount of risk.

If we have good discernment skills, meaning we have the tools to sort the wheat from the chaff, chances are we'll have good reality testing. This good discernment is helped along by the conviction that we trust what we see is real. By contrast, if you don't trust your ability to accurately see what's in front of you, you may hinder yourself from making good decisions. This process won't flow smoothly if it involves undue anxiety, because that will definitely cloud your vision.

Sometimes we want to believe something is true so much that we ignore evidence that proves otherwise. Sometimes our fears are so strong they push us to the most egregious, but false, conclusions. Good reality testing involves finding the balance between the two extremes and seeing things for how they truly are.

Impulse control is the ability to be patient, persevere and delay future gratification. It's also the ability to restrain yourself from reacting to intense, emotional triggers. When people have good impulse control, I usually find they also have good boundaries and know their limits. When people have good impulse control, they can appropriately govern, contain and manage their emotions. Instead of their reactions controlling them, we could say they have control over their responses and they can resist the temptation to react inappropriately.

From the work of Susan Johnson, a clinical psychologist who researches adult emotional attachment, anger is actually a secondary emotion, not a primary one. For those who are quick to anger, it may help them to remember that what they're really feeling isn't anger, but most likely one of these emotions: fear, sadness, shame, guilt, embarrassment or hurt. Stopping and taking a pause to assess what you're really feeling before reacting may prevent you from saying or doing something you could regret later.

I often notice that when someone has low impulse control, they also have an addictive personality or even a trauma background. In my experience, this is often because the person has a low threshold for emotional pain and wants to escape or avoid emotionally charged situations. If this is the case, the person has to work through their addiction to strengthen their impulse control. This requires a mind shift, and the person has to consciously choose to find integrity in a life lived in reality more than an escape to fantasy.

Sometimes we may want something to be true so badly we ignore data to the contrary. For example, you want your boss to like you. Every day, as your boss walks by your office, she smiles and speaks pleasantly. You feel reassured and believe everything is OK. However, you ignore her critical comments about your presentations and reports. By ignoring this conflicting data, you miss the chance to recognize the need for corrective action.

At other times, we become blinded by our fears. Again, you want your boss to like you but fear she doesn't. One day, she walks by without speaking, so you conclude she hates you. The truth is she has a headache, is absorbed in her own thoughts or is totally clueless about other people's feelings – take your pick. You failed to consider alternative explanations for your data because of your intense fears.

Whenever we interact with someone, we make up a story or a theory in our head about what their behavior means. People do this all the time. Those with strong reality testing abilities recognize their theories are just theories. They obtain data to substantiate or disprove their theories because people are complicated and the capacity for us to misunderstand each other is infinite.

In addition, poor reality testing abilities can lead to serious misinterpretations of critical business data. Whether we like it or not, emotions can have an impact on the way we view the numbers. Excessive fear can lead someone to react negatively to certain numbers and miss an opportunity that our competitors find.

Overly rosy views of business possibilities can also cause problems. If data that comes in isn't what we hoped or promised someone it would be, we may be tempted to underestimate the true meaning of the data. Letting your hopes sway your judgment won't make it so.

Emotions express themselves through three channels – thoughts, physical sensations and the impulses we experience to translate the feelings into behavior. When sad, most people have the impulse to cry. When angry, people usually have the impulse to say something ugly or even to hit. Impulse control involves having good command over when we allow our emotions to be expressed in our behavior. Good control requires an intervening thought that measures and judges the consequence of turning the impulse into action.

When impulses are translated directly into behavior, we call it acting out the feeling represented by the impulse. People behave impulsively, without thinking through the consequences, when the pressure of emotion builds up beyond their ability to inhibit unwise behavior. People with strong impulse control can restrain their actions until they have time to think, even in response to intense emotional pressure.

Frank's Story

Frank was a South Carolina lawyer trained by the Charleston School of Law. Strong and stocky, he stood 6'2" tall, with black wavy hair and brown eyes. When he spoke I could hear the magnolia trees in his voice, and I wondered what it would be like to be in the courtroom listening to him litigate in his genteel drawl.

Frank came to me to get unstuck at work. "I'm no longer getting satisfaction from my career, and I don't know what to do," he told me. An avid tennis player, he fantasized about quitting work altogether and playing tournaments instead.

He lacked clarity, and didn't know what type of work would bring him satisfaction and fulfillment. One thing was clear to him and we started there: He didn't like the experience of working for the people he worked with; plus, they were close family friends, so staying or leaving the firm was more complicated by this dual relationship. In addition, he didn't want to continue doing what he labeled mundane work, where he had no influence to effect or execute major initiatives.

The Evaluation

We began by taking a career history. By asking questions and listening to his answers, I found learned patterns peppered his entire story:

- He always felt passed over for well-deserved promotions and additional responsibilities.

- He always felt he was treated unfairly.

- He never felt acknowledged, affirmed or rewarded for his accomplishments.

- He's been disenchanted for years with his career, despite the fact he had a law degree from a prestigious school and had worked for reputable law firms in admiralty and maritime law.

In short, Frank felt inadequate, albeit disempowered, and asked me to help him sort out his next career steps to break out of what he referred to as his rut. I was unsure it was really a rut, as it sounded to me like a continuous and predictable pattern of disengagement with life. I withheld my opinion though, as I knew it would most likely come across as unsupportive to him at this early point in our work together.

Instead, I helped him focus on reflecting on his career and identifying the high points, including his professional strengths. "I've never been able to put a finger on what makes me happy," he told me while doing this exercise. "I need to be wanted, valued and influential at my job, which is something I haven't experienced before."

After these first few meetings, Frank emailed me and said he felt encouraged by our conversations and felt he was making progress. He said that at our next meeting, he wanted to talk about his concept of fairness and his inability to stick up for himself and confront challenging people at work. "Think about what qualities you see in the people you admire most," I responded. "These would be the ones you most want to emulate."

"I don't like confrontation so I don't tell people I don't like how they're treating me," he told me. "I also don't like to disappoint people. Also, when something's unfair, I feel like someone further up the totem pole should fix it."

"By believing this, you're surrendering your own authority and selling yourself short," I explained to Frank, who didn't understand this concept, and told me more stories about how other people had disrupted and ruined his career.

Frank asked me how he could recognize his own authority and stand up for himself. I questioned him about his need for approval, which he acknowledged as a driving force behind his quietude. He said he wanted to go back to being a positive person, yet when I asked him to recall a time in his life when he was that way, he couldn't. He shared his fear that he'd be regretful at the end of his life, citing more examples of how people failed to value him, how he suffered through his daily work life while trying to make the best of it, and how no one recognized him for the professional strengths he brought to the table. I was very surprised at our next meeting when he told me it was cathartic and beneficial to go through his career timeline, because I thought it was actually very taxing for him.

Frank also told me his wife wasn't excited he was seeing a career coach. "I think my wife has trained me to dampen my natural enthusiasm when she's not excited about something new I want to do," he told me. "I'm an idea person who gets excited about the potential and promise of a new initiative."

The Work

Frank liked solving problems by coming up with new ideas and wanted a job where he could express his creativity. "I'm interested in innovation and helping entrepreneurs give birth to their new ideas," he said.

Part of his career history, though, was working for a startup in Charleston's NoMo Corridor that didn't succeed. He enjoyed that job but didn't like the constant stress wondering how the firm would make payroll every month, so he eventually left for a more stable environment.

I asked Frank to do at-home assignments. He'd been having networking coffees to meet people and investigate different career possibilities. Since he didn't like the people he worked with, I asked him to make a list of qualities he'd like his coworkers to possess. He wasn't sure he was making progress, so I asked him to define what progress looked like to him and how to know when he was making progress.

I recommended Frank read the book, *Trust Your Life: Forgive Yourself and Go After Your Dreams* by Noelle Sterne, because it contains true, inspirational stories about people who radically changed their lives and careers, becoming successful and happy in the process. To further motivate and inspire him, I asked him to research and listen to podcasts of successful people and their stories.

Because Frank was having trouble tolerating his anxiety, I shared tools with him designed to help soothe scary thoughts. I suggested he use a concept called mind mapping, which is similar to flow charting, and jot down different possibilities for his next career steps to stimulate his creativity.

To help Frank reframe his negative thoughts and think more positively, I showed him how to use affirmations, which are positive statements in the present tense as though he had already accomplished his dreams. Examples are: "I know, accept and am true to myself" and "I never give up."

I asked him to get a journal and write out his thoughts and feelings on a daily basis so we could track his progress and look for patterns. "I wish this process of figuring out what I want would be easier than this," Frank told me.

Some of the activities he found exciting, like meeting with people for coffee and hearing about their work, and some he found tedious, such as defining what success looked like to him. He experienced both the highs and the lows typical of this type of work.

It took many meetings before Frank agreed to take the EQ-i 2.0 leadership assessment. When he did, he scored very high in some skills and very low in others, which meant he was very out of balance in his skillset. Whenever someone scores 10 points higher or lower in one skill vs. another in this model he or she won't be in balance. When that happens, we need to work to help him or her balance out all skills so they can be more effective. In this way, high scores can actually give low results when not balanced by the other skills. For instance, Frank scored very high in problem solving and very low in reality testing and impulse control.

This means when it comes to problem solving, Frank might ignore his feelings entirely when making decisions (he also scored very low in emotional self-awareness), seem cold or impersonal when presenting solutions to others, and fixate on a problem, obsessing about it, when he can't see a ready solution. When I questioned Frank about the efficacy of these three scenarios, he said they did indeed apply to him. I pointed out to him that even though he felt like he didn't know what he wanted, there were some things he knew about himself: For example, in the Decision-Making Composite, he scored highest in problem solving. This confirmed his own experience, because he told me several times he enjoyed finding solutions to problems.

However, the results told us why he wasn't an effective decision maker: He scored very low in reality testing and impulse control, the other two skills in the Decision-Making Composite. To be effective at making good decisions, he'd need to build these two skills and have them be in balance with his problem-solving skills.

These results helped me have another discussion with Frank to poke holes in his belief that the world was unfair. I suggested that since his score was so low in reality testing, his emotions were getting in the way of him seeing situations objectively as they really are and that instead, he saw himself as a victim. I strongly suggested this wasn't an accurate self-appraisal.

"I agree that I need to view my work life with more perspective," Frank said, and mentioned receiving feedback from others that he had "bad discernment skills."

What did this really mean for him in terms of how he made decisions at work? Although he was good at intuiting good strategy, he was at high risk for getting derailed by his own emotions. When he thought he was being treated unfairly, he got triggered by his own anger, which translated into physical symptoms: His hands balled up into fists, his chest got tight, his heart beat faster, and he had panic attacks.

This physical tension would actually prevent him from expressing his opinions in a meeting. While in this state, he avoided confrontation because he didn't deal well with discord. His lack of patience rendered him ineffective. This reaction was something Frank wanted to change because it made him feel like a coward and had a negative effect on his self-regard.

It was a big part of what was holding him back because when this happened, his own emotional upset would hold him hostage for hours and sometimes all day long. Frank sat and stewed over what happened to him and how unfair it all was, and this would feed and fuel his anger and upset. This behavior was futile because although he ruminated over every detail that occurred, he failed to see his part in things. That meant he had no clue how to change the predictable transactions that occurred because he underestimated his own sense of agency.

Since Frank got emotionally tense and tight so often, he had trouble sleeping and often woke in the morning unrefreshed. I asked him to visit his doctor to rule out any physical reasons for his sleep disturbances and anxiety. I worked with him on the emotional reasons by helping him build his patience, or impulse control, and using mindfulness tools to decrease his anxiety and stress.

I encouraged him to journal as much as possible to cope with his feelings of stress. Since I know the antidote to anxiety is to gather information and take action steps, we formulated a strategic plan for his career explorations. One of the development goals was for Frank to nurture his relationships with family, friends and himself. Since one of the things that was so important to Frank was his happiness and well-being, it was pivotal he focus on having fun and participating in restorative activities, too. This was especially true as he continued to struggle with physical stress symptoms: pains in his shoulder blades, his neck, headaches and more.

Frank agreed it was important he be less impulsive. "I'm making efforts to listen to what other people are saying before trying to finish their sentences," he told me.

He found listening to podcasts on the science of success, making commitments and taking action, and changing mindsets to be an important adjunct to our meetings. Listening to them in between our talking times helped keep him focused. He needed this supplemental support because there was a lot of back and forth in his progress.

Because it was uncomfortable for Frank to face that he wasn't where he wanted to be in his life, personally or professionally, it was difficult for him to dialogue about it with me. He wanted to avoid his emotional discomfort at all costs, and he went off on tangents. Though I could follow the threads of the real issue no matter what subject he brought up, I reeled him back in to help refocus his thoughts on the main issue and face it squarely. In this way, he experienced himself as being more focused. Once he knew what that felt like, he'd have a template in his brain for the experience and it would start to build the neural pathway, making it easier for him to return there on his own.

As part of the back-and-forth progress, sometimes we had to slow our discussions down because of Frank's physical symptoms. When they became too intense, we switched gears and worked on a different subject. If felt like dancing to me: We balanced our discussions with his physical symptoms and doctor visits. When the panic symptoms like dizziness, chest pain and headaches became more pronounced, we backed off and Frank visited his doctor.

When the physical symptoms died off, we forged ahead more assertively. I was satisfied we were on the right path because Frank's doctor consistently assured him he could find no physical reason for his upsets: He wasn't in danger of having a heart attack or stroke. This news concerned Frank because he wanted to know the reasons for his anxiety and from his point of view, they eluded him. "I want to know the answers to a lot of my questions: What's my career dream?" he told me. "What would make me feel happy and successful? How do I know if I'm changing? How do I put things into perspective? I remember myself as a happy-go-lucky kid, so what happened?"

At this point in our work we went back to looking at how Frank established his definition of personal and professional success. We talked about the different people he admired and how he developed the standards and expectations he set for himself based on these specific role models. Together we discovered some were healthy standards and expectations to strive for and some weren't.

I gave Frank more homework and asked him to write down significant events in his life and examine the various emotions he attached to those events. At our next meeting, he told me he had trouble defining more than two emotions. "I had to look up a list of emotions on Wikipedia for ideas," he said. This made sense to me: Because he also scored low in emotional self-awareness, it was often hard for him to accurately know what he was actually feeling. We could say his internal guidance system was turned off.

When I offered him this insight, he disagreed with me: "I believe in myself and don't think there's such a thing as an internal guidance system to help me figure out what I want in life."

In the same way Frank didn't know what emotion he was feeling, he didn't know what he wanted to do with his life, so he wasn't committed to any particular course of action. His ambivalence and lack of self-awareness was evident in these comments he made: "that he felt driven to pursue things he didn't really want and he got fatigued thinking about things he really didn't want to do." I attempted to spur his creativity to help him generate the energy to find his true calling. I invited him to think about his career development as something he was exploring rather than something he was trying to pinpoint.

I thought that would lift the burden of obligation he was carrying and reframe it as something that was more adventurous and fun. Despite the fact he was slow to catch on, Frank persevered and eventually told me he was becoming more comfortable with the uncertainty, or the "not knowing," and the freedom of being able to explore. His exploring paid off and one of the new things he did was to join an executive board for a nonprofit in an area of interest that was outside of his normal expertise so he stretched himself past his comfort zone.

The Results

Over time, Frank made progress speaking his opinions in meetings and taking a more direct stance in his conversations at work. In turn, he started feeling more effective, and this motivated him to continue. He even noticed he started feeling proud of his skills; he recognized his own accomplishments more frequently. These positive feelings gave him the courage to submit a proposal for legal consulting work with a firm he met while doing his coffee networking meetings. The company's mission and vision seemed more exciting and challenging, and he was happy when his proposal was accepted. After the initial excitement wore off, it was replaced by anxiety about whether or not he'd actually like this new job. We worked through this anxiety once he actually got started.

Frank had a moment of internal awareness and made the comment that committing to this was difficult for him. I interpreted his new consciousness as progress and forward movement. The fact that he was putting a stake in the ground and trying something new was a true act of courage for him. He was taking this action in spite of having nagging doubts. "I'm not enjoying this investigation of my self-awareness, feelings or my career," he told me. "It's not my true nature to be self-reflective or investigational." He repeated this over the next few meetings, saying he wanted to be done soon.

After taking this new job, he reported he was no longer burdened by heavy thoughts and felt less physical tension on a daily basis. Although he was apprehensive before starting, once he was there he had more energy and the time passed quickly. He understood what was required of him and felt comfortable in his new role. He also felt his role as a legal consultant was helping him have a new understanding of his skills and accomplishments. He noticed this new awareness allowed him to speak up more and take a more direct approach in his communications with direct reports and colleagues than was previously possible for him.

While doing the same work in a new context, Frank recognized the traits and skills he valued about himself: being people-oriented, problem solving, opportunity-creating and unstructured. To reinforce his new awareness – and because he wanted to be sure he was doing what he was meant to be doing – I asked him to keep reflecting on where he's already successful in his life and spend more time focusing on those stories.

Frank did this, and said this created significant change in his life as he was able to keep expressing himself more and more, appropriately, of course, without being so concerned with the consequences. He learned to take a stand for himself without needing other people's approval, which was a major step in advancing his self-regard.

Building Your Reality Testing and Impulse Control

Building your reality testing can help you conserve mental and emotional energy. It can help you redirect your energy into focused strategic planning, which will empower you, instead of compelling you down a rabbit hole. It can also help you keep your head clear, and your relationships intact. No direct report, peer or boss enjoys being misread or having their actions misinterpreted by your unconscious bias, positive or negative. If you develop your reality testing, you'll be better able to notice and identify the right actions you need to take and those you don't to elicit the greatest impact on your success and well-being. Impulsive behavior can undo in seconds what it took weeks, months or even years for you to build or establish.

Sometimes it can wipe out the trust two people have for each other. Reckless behavior can cause someone to quit a good job prematurely because he's angry at the boss, or leave a fulfilling relationship because his feelings were hurt over a misunderstanding.

When I was in training for my Ed.S. in Marriage and Family Therapy, my supervisor Jenelle Spear ingrained into my head that it's often better to err on the side of caution than impulse. Her words of wisdom have consistently steered me in the right direction.

Feel free to borrow them and liberate yourself from knee-jerk reactions. Slow down the reptile brain, stop to think, and you'll often find a better response.

Exercises for Exploration and Mastery: Reality Testing and Impulse Control

Remember while acting out an impulse can involve either good or bad behaviors, it's the bad behavior that's usually associated with the term. Acting out, and the damage that often results, is what has given emotions a bad reputation in Western philosophy, as articulated by the Stoics like Marcus Aurelius, as well as Descartes and Voltaire. Learning to manage the power of our own emotions can open up an untapped reservoir of effectiveness. The energy that fuels impulsive behavior is the same energy, that when controlled better, motivates us to high achievement. Work on these exercises to learn more about your reality testing and impulse control.

Exercise 1

Think of a situation where you became intensely, emotionally charged. Did you react or respond? Did you feel something in your body warning you your reptile brain was going from zero to 100 in a split second? What did you feel? Some common signals are butterflies in the stomach, a lump in the throat or a rapid heartbeat. Write out the story of how you reacted or responded. Review what worked and what didn't.

Your Takeaway: Consider these questions. What were the consequences of your actions? What do you wish you could improve? If you had to do it over again, what would you do differently?

Exercise 2

When you have an emotionally charged reaction, stop before you act. If you need to have a conversation with someone, write it out or bullet the main points before you say or do anything. Read through this script again and take out any emotionally charged words that the other person could react defensively to and attempt to make what you're conveying as emotion-free as possible.

Your Takeaway: State your intention and just the facts rather than your interpretations.

Exercise 3

Sit in your emotions and let them pass. The next time you feel called to hurry up and lash out, or feel a sense of urgency to speak out in anger or passion, it might make sense to stop and think first. Try to sit in your emotion and identify what you're truly feeling: sadness, fear, hurt, shame, guilt or embarrassment. Ask yourself if you can hold and contain these feelings rather than pass them along like a hot potato to someone else you're angry with; then, attempt to trace these feelings back to the first time you ever felt them.

Your Takeaway: Remember, your interpretations about the present moment are skewed because of an event that happened in the past.

Exercise 4

Reflect on addictive behaviors. If you have an addiction that's causing you to pursue reckless behavior, reach out to a professional and ask for help. Are you in this type of situation and are you ready to ask for help?

Your Takeaway: You'll have to work on the addiction to build your impulse control.

Exercise 5

The next time you're called upon to size up a situation at work, back up and see the big picture. Is your decision-making style leading you to make decisions out of worst-case-scenario thinking or avoidance? Step back and gather evidence, and dispute and debate the negative self-talk in your head.

Your Takeaway: Talk yourself down from any emotions and self-soothe by using supportive self-talk: Talk to yourself as a loving, helpful parent would. This will help you approach the decision in a more clear-headed way.

Exercise 6

Look at your independence score if you took the EQ-i 2.0 assessment. How high was it? Be aware that sometimes people who score low in independence have more trouble with reality testing, because they lack the confidence to implement their decision.

Your Takeaway: If this is true about you, go back to the exercises on independence and work on that skill first.

Exercise 7

Look at your stress tolerance score if you took the EQ-i 2.0 assessment. Sometimes, people who score low in impulse control also score low in stress tolerance.

Your Takeaway: If you think this is true of you, go to the exercises on stress tolerance and work those first.

Exercise 8

Look at the times when you think you behaved impulsively. Reflect on how those situations make you feel now.

Your Takeaway: After you've reviewed your patterns and triggers, address them and find a way to behave differently next time.

Part V

Stress Management Composite

Story One: Cindy

stress tolerance: the ability to withstand adverse
events and stressful situations without "falling apart" by
actively and positively coping with stress.

Does this sound familiar? You arrive at your desk at 9 a.m., and instead of catching up on conversation over coffee with a coworker, you're sitting white-knuckled, looking at your to-do list, which seems a mile long and totally insurmountable.

A colleague comes over and asks how you're doing. You throw your hands up into the air and exclaim, "I'm freaking out! I'm going to be taking files home tonight and working till midnight! There's no way I'm going to be able to get all of these projects done. No way!"

How do you think your colleague will respond? It's a great colleague who'll sit down and listen to a vent fest. More likely, the person will put their own hands up, back away and say they have to get back to their own work. It's tough to deal with another person's visible, frustrated work stress.

Let's say you took a different approach. You really do have a lot of work and conflicting deadlines. You could approach your boss and ask her to help you prioritize and shift deadlines. You could also ask for help from other team members to get out of the crunch. You could ask a trusted colleague for some insight on how to juggle your workload in a more efficient way.

Although stress can be synonymous with the workplace, we could argue some occupations are more stressful than others. When you're required to meet sales quotas, goals or fixed deadlines, you're rolling the dice and taking major risks, so there will always be an element of stress.

How well you address and deal with your stressors is what separates you from average or low performers, and makes you a star.

When you face a major challenge, do you fall apart emotionally? Do you get anxious, tense or irritable? Do you affect others negatively by snapping at them? Do you catastrophize, always imagining the worst-case scenario? If so, you're behaving in a low emotionally intelligent way.

However, if you meet difficulties head on, taking action to keep yourself grounded while making steady, measured progress, then you're behaving in a highly emotionally intelligent manner. Most likely, you're also behaving in a level-headed way and can assess circumstances objectively.

Having good stress tolerance means you know how to self-soothe and pace yourself, so you stay clear-headed under pressure. The most effective leaders hold up under extreme stress, without letting intense emotions get the best of them or cloud their judgment.

Having poor stress tolerance often leads to physical symptoms such as rapid heartbeat, migraines or tension headaches, heartburn or digestive problems, insomnia, weight gain, or even high blood pressure. If you want to live a high-quality life, it's smart to learn how to calm your mind and deal with hard times gracefully.

Poor stress tolerance can also lead to escapist behaviors, such as smoking, drinking, gambling, compulsive shopping or eating disorders. Research indicates that left unchecked, stress can actually kill us – or at least lead us down the path of self-defeating behaviors.

Since having low stress tolerance can interfere with reality testing, flexibility and impulse control, it is important for professionals to assess their own skills. Developing high stress tolerance helps to create a sense of personal empowerment or high self-regard, good problem solving, and a belief that you can influence needed change as a leader.

One of the dangers of feeling overwhelmed by stress can be that it encourages you to take a passive stance. In many situations, at work and at home, being proactive is usually more adaptive, makes us feel better, and may save our jobs, relationships and lives.

If you're assessing yourself with low stress tolerance right now, the good news is that you can learn to face stress in a positive way, without falling apart.

Cindy's Story

When Cindy first visited my office, she reminded me of a skittish colt ready to bolt at the first opportunity – it seemed she didn't really want to meet with me, but endured our sessions despite her apparent discomfort. That impressed me about her immediately.

Cindy was 28, and had long brown hair and green eyes. She was from California and had earned a degree in finance from Stanford University. Her favorite hobby was going to dog agility shows with her puppy, Gia.

Cindy came to see me because she wanted to get promoted at the bank where she worked - and her addiction to online gambling and compulsive shopping was getting in the way of her career advancement. Online gambling and shopping was all she could think about, even at work.

"I'm pretty sure my managers can tell I'm on my phone a lot and not totally paying attention in team meetings," she told me. "My marriage is also suffering. My husband says he feels lonely and single."

Cindy started her career in mortgage lending and eventually became a top producer. Her job was 100% sales, and since she was an extrovert, it was a good fit. In addition, she scored high in interpersonal relationships and empathy, which explained her job success there. Mortgage lending felt good to Cindy because she made a sale every day, and this was an accomplishment toward her annual production goals.

Seeking more opportunity for future advancement, she transitioned about a year ago from the mortgage company to her current position in asset-based lending, working with struggling businesses. Because this was a different part of the bank, located at its headquarters, it was like starting over for Cindy. At this job, she held a backroom position analyzing data. Since it wasn't as people-oriented and she was over-qualified, she felt bored.

Cindy had been waiting for an opening in a development program that would qualify her for a higher-level position as a business development officer with exposure to the public. The company posted openings annually and candidates were accepted by invitation only. Although she said her boss "loved her," and considered her ambitious and motivated, he couldn't guarantee her a spot in the class. If she did get accepted into the development class, it would give her a clearer advancement path. Without clarity, she lacked confidence that she'd land the job she wanted, doing something she loved and using her gifts and talents.

She thought some of her friends seemed happier than her. "I thought I'd be making more money than I am now," Cindy told me. "I feel constant insecurity because I'm not doing as well as I think I should be doing. I should be at the officer level now and I'm still an associate, so if nothing changes in a year I may look for something else."

Cindy reported to me that she suffered from "slight" anxiety so her doctor gave her a prescription for Lexapro to use when needed. She worried about making a mistake "by accident" or "breaking a rule" because she was constantly checking her phone for the latest gambling information on a site called Starburst. Her anxiety and panic attacks surfaced when she underwent big changes, like a new job. In addition to her anxiety Cindy had been diagnosed with an impulse control disorder in high school, so it was harder for her to stay focused.

The Evaluation

When we discussed her cross-addiction to online gambling and compulsive shopping, Cindy said, "Anything can trigger me, like seeing a Macy's catalog or a lottery ticket at a convenience store." Since her husband worked in the medical field, he got up earlier than Cindy and was often exhausted by the time she got home. He went to bed earlier than she did. Recently, he told her he'd like her to come to bed earlier so he wouldn't feel so alone in the marriage. This made Cindy more anxious, because she didn't know how she'd be able to change her habits and accommodate her husband's request. This gave her another thing to ruminate about, even while at work.

Cindy came from a family where she had a lot to live up to: Her father owned his own medical practice and several of her siblings worked in it. She also said her father put a lot of pressure on her to be successful, and she often felt a false sense of confidence. I could see this in her fast-paced manner of speaking and her way of quickly dismissing certain hypotheses of mine, as though she never gave them even a moment's thought

Cindy often got cranky as a result of being anxious at work, and people didn't like that side of her. "I don't like not to be liked," Cindy told me. This clue helped me identify when she was anxious in our meetings, but also unaware of this behavior.

She described her family as hard-core doctors, where it was expected that she and all her siblings attend the same high-profile medical university. Although she applied, she didn't get into that school and that really upset her at the time. She said her parents put a lot of pressure on her to get accepted into a medical program, and this affected her long-term view of herself.

During our work together, we found this old script was still playing in her head and affecting her sense of accomplishment. Mortgage banking and asset-based lending weren't medical fields. I wondered if Cindy needed to redefine her definition of success on her own terms, instead of accepting those of her family.

Cindy's father was a doctor, and her mother was the dean of a nursing school. Both parents were highly successful in their own right, and they flourished in academics. Cindy's father graduated top of his class, and her mother held two Ph.D. degrees, so they expected a lot from their children. All of their children excelled at academics, except for Cindy. This was a significant factor in Cindy's self-assessment that she wasn't thriving or excelling as much as her siblings.

This contributed to her low sense of self-regard, and set her up to continuously escape reality through online buying and gambling whenever she was stressed by anxious thoughts and negative self-talk. One more factor is important here: Cindy tried out for track in college, but didn't make the team. This was a significant disappointment for her at the time. I suspected it was a factor in her obsession with online gambling: She wanted to redeem herself by winning and feeling successful.

In addition to the tension Cindy was experiencing at work, she was getting a double dose of it at home. Things came to a head one evening with her husband, when he asked her for help folding five loads of laundry. Although she told him she'd be right there to assist him, she couldn't resist placing a bet on her phone first. She got so involved in his pursuit that she didn't realize 45 minutes had passed by and her husband had already finished the laundry by himself and gone to bed.

"I'm starting to realize my behavior is creating emotional distance in my marriage and I want to change it," Cindy told me. "I want to stop staying up late at night placing bets or buying clothes while my husband goes to bed early by himself."

In addition, she told me that at work she was nodding off in more meetings, not focusing or concentrating well. "I don't like the way I'm behaving and am starting to have some insights into the consequences it's creating at work and at home," she said.

The Work

Before we could tackle Cindy's workplace anxiety, we worked on her self-defeating, negative habit patterns first. This was the origin of her discomfort. It's my experience that healthy self-regard has to be in place before you begin addressing and building stress tolerance. Cindy's behavior caused her to feel shame, negatively affecting her confidence.

There are many good methods for changing negative behavior patterns and we used them all: hypnosis, journaling, mindfulness, demystifying the past and using the ABCDE exercise (it's at the back of this book) to identify and reframe triggers.

Cindy was remarkable because she elected to extinguish the behavior cold turkey, despite the fact I told her usually a very small percentage of people are able to do this and sustain the behavior change. According to Dr. Reuven Bar-On's model, you need to change thoughts and feelings to create long-term behavioral change. In my opinion, this remarkable cold stop happened because Cindy was ready to make a big change.

Cindy was mentally and emotionally committed, which is a necessary prerequisite for any type of genuine change. One of her top priorities was to not let her husband down. She was motivated because her relationship with her husband felt better than ever as a result of stopping her negative behavior. Instead of staying up late to shop alone or place bets, she started going to bed when her husband went to bed and was getting better sleep consistently.

"I feel closer to my husband emotionally," Cindy told me. "I'm fully present when I'm with him and he tells me he feels paid attention to and acknowledged. One of our favorite things to do is to take long walks together, and this helps us bond emotionally."

Cindy felt like a better partner and wife. She also noticed benefits at work: She was more alert in meetings, she felt less isolated and she was building a solid rapport with her coworkers.

To support the full cessation of her negative behavior, we added a couple of tools. I wasn't fully convinced Cindy's change was deep and long lasting, as opposed to temporary and situational. As if to support this hypothesis, we noticed Cindy's craving for certain foods and eating increased, and we had to watch her food intake because she didn't want to gain weight.

Cindy started keeping a journal to track her moods and feelings throughout the day. She later included food intake and exercise so she could better monitor her weight. However, then she started having intense cravings for sugar, mostly triggered during social occasions with friends and family.

Here's my point: Until we could get to the bottom of what caused Cindy's anxiety in the first place, addictive-like behaviors would continue to pop up like popcorn. Although the form a behavior takes can morph from one type of expression to another, the behavior masks a pattern we'd need to identify to totally stop the negative behaviors.

At this point in the program Cindy didn't agree with me. I suggested doing the EQ-i 2.0 assessment so we could see where she was in and out of balance on specific skills. She believed that because she was able to stop behaviors that had controlled her for 13 years so quickly, and practically overnight, they were gone forever and she needed to do nothing more.

While I like to hold space for the fact this could be true, I'd never seen it work this way during my 16 years doing this work. Because the stakes were so high, I shared this with Cindy, even though I knew the chances were huge that she wouldn't be able to hear me. Cindy became defensive and angry, and left without making another appointment. I worried about having offended her and hoped we had enough of a positive relationship built up that she'd feel free to return.

Luckily, I didn't have to wait long. Cindy returned within a couple of weeks. Dealing with stressful family issues provoked another panic attack and she realized there was more work to do. She didn't want to gamble with losing ground we had already covered. She decided she wanted to work on her emotional intelligence skills after all.

I pointed out that our relationship survived a heated discussion and then a resistant retreat, after which she felt the freedom to return. The fact that she could get past these previous obstacles signaled to me she was truly ready to continue.

That's why the next step of our program involved taking the EQ-i 2.0 workplace assessment. Cindy's lowest score on the assessment was in the Stress Management Composite, specifically in stress tolerance. In addition, this score was out of balance with both flexibility and optimism, in which she scored highest. With both her highest and lowest scores being in the Stress Management Composite, and with them being out of balance (more than 10 points apart), it was no surprise to me that this was a difficult area for Cindy. By balancing these three subscales, I expected to see impressive improvements for her.

We started identifying aspects of Cindy's life that triggered stress reactions. These are some of the past and current stressors she identified, most involving an element of negative self-talk:

- Fear of not hitting her production and sales goals

- Worries about whether the deal she's working on will go through or not

- Worries about getting fired

- Wonders whether she can handle rejection and failure

- Wonders whether she can handle success

- Worries about how to structure her day

- Wonders whether she can achieve work-life balance

- Watching the family dog run around anxiously.

When we explored the topic of fear of failure, Cindy told a story of how she originally failed her SAFE mortgage loan officer exam and had to retake it three times before passing. This caused her to lose her job at a previous mortgage company, but she quickly found another one she liked better. After that, she was a consistent top producer and always made her production volume goals. While we learned that some of her fears were valid and based on true past experiences, we also learned she survived them and was able to move forward. Acknowledging this helped build trust in herself, her abilities and her self-regard.

Cindy enjoyed being motivated by a sense of fear because she was a ballet dancer as a child, and that's how her dance teachers motivated her. I don't believe fear-based motivation creates sustainable behavior change because it doesn't evoke changing thoughts and feelings. Instead, I use approaches that channel my client's fear and anxiety in more positive directions by taking action.

The Results

Here are some of the positive steps we took for homework: Cindy really benefited from journaling so I asked her to write out the mortgage loan officer exam story in an attempt to unravel it and understand what happened. Then I asked her to write about her sales job at the retail branch and how she consistently met her goals year after year. I requested she pay close attention to the fact that she could count on herself, and the confident feeling that generated, to consistently carry out the tasks necessary to achieve her goals.

Then I suggested Cindy see herself as being able to take the steps necessary to produce the goals she needed to meet in her current job: to realize that if she did it before, she can do it again. She already had a success template in her mind. In other words, her skills hadn't changed, just the context. I also asked her to visualize herself in the development class daily, using a closed-eye process and incorporating as many of her five senses as possible.

I suggested she write out a mission and vision statement for herself, as though she were a corporation. I asked her to read the book, *The Five Love Languages* by Gary Chapman. This communication method can be used at home and at work to build relationships with family and colleagues. I also asked Cindy to study the 16 EQ-i 2.0 skill definitions to better understand them.

One of the key factors was to find a way for Cindy to handle the boredom and lack of fulfillment she felt on a daily basis at her job. I suggested she look for creative ways to find interesting things to do, such as going on prospecting calls with a colleague. Since prospecting involved contact with people outside her regular work environment and it stimulated her need to meet new people as an extrovert, she started to feel more relaxed at work and now goes out of her way to connect to and talk with her colleagues.

As we worked to bring Cindy's anxieties about workplace success within a manageable range, she no longer needed Lexapro. Doing the homework exercises energized her on a daily basis and her cravings for snacks and food diminished. Maintaining her weight helped build her self-regard. As we expanded her daily repertoire of creative ways to build connection with colleagues at work, her need to relate to people was satisfied and she became more flexible.

Cindy used her emotional self-awareness to be more mindful of when she was becoming anxious. When this happened, she used one of the tools in her toolkit to appropriately calm herself. She felt more in control managing her fear thoughts and runaway emotions. This helped her appear less "cranky" to coworkers and her working relationships became more fluid and predictable. She started getting more positive feedback from her boss and peers, balancing out her Stress Management Composite.

The best part of this story is that Cindy scored the promotion to business development officer, and is currently flourishing and exceeding expectations for production and sales goals.

Building Your Stress Tolerance

I like to think of having good stress tolerance skills as being poised, and having grace under pressure. Some people are very skilled at containing, managing and controlling their emotional expression, and others aren't.

Can you think of someone you know who's not self-possessed when it comes to his emotions? If so, think about how it feels to be around him when there's a crisis. Does he inspire you to take action or does he frazzle your nerves? Does he draw you closer or does his behaviors push you away?

Now think about someone who has it all together and is the epitome of grace and poise. How do you feel around her when there's a crisis brewing? How are these feelings the same or different than the other example?

Which one of these two people would you prefer to be like? My guess is you'd rather emulate the person who can appropriately govern her emotions because she'll be able to guide you safely through difficulties. In the clinical world, this is referred to as maintaining a calm, non-anxious presence. In this EQ-i 2.0 model, it's about having good stress tolerance.

Since our bodies are so closely tied with our emotional states, it's helpful to have a method to diffuse stress from your body. There are many methods and techniques available for this, and I'll discuss some in the exercises below. See if you can find the one method that speaks to you; otherwise, your coach can help you learn stress tolerance skills or help you find other resources.

Exercises for Exploration and Mastery: Stress Tolerance

Stress tolerance exercises work best if you practice them every day, because they rely on repetition to effectively reprogram your unconscious mind.

Exercise 1

Take three deep breaths. The next time you're in a stressful situation, try taking three deep breaths to reset your autonomic nervous system. Breathe deeply from your belly. You'll know you're doing it right when you notice your stomach expanding out and contracting. This will have the benefit of calming you down. How does deep breathing make you feel?

Your Takeaway: Try to notice how you felt before you took your deep breaths, and compare that to how you felt afterward. Do you notice any difference?

Exercise 2

Learn how to meditate. It's easy to find information on how to meditate, including apps you can use if you don't want to take a long course of study. With some of them, you can decide how long you wish to meditate. While some serious devotees spend several hours a day in meditation, that isn't necessary for building stress tolerance. How does meditating make you feel?

Your Takeaway: Even if you only have a few minutes a day, taking a timeout will help you learn to calm and soothe the reptile brain.

Exercise 3

Practice mindfulness. If you want to take a class, or read a book, look for one that explores mindfulness, which is the practice of being present and centered in the here and now, as opposed to the past or the future. What does mindfulness mean to you?

Your Takeaway: Practicing mindfulness can improve your ability to focus and concentrate. It can help you truly listen and be present to another person.

Exercise 4

Practice your gratitude. Recent research has demonstrated that when people focus on naming or writing down three things a day they're grateful for, it helps them feel more abundant and happy.

Your Takeaway: Some people even keep a separate gratitude journal for this daily practice.

Exercise 5

Count to 10. While this may sound old hat, it really works and here's why. Counting to 10 in a stressful situation helps to deactivate the flight-or-fight response by slowing down the reptile brain. The reptile brain is quick to trigger, and can go from zero to 100 in a split second. You might say or do something you later regret. The antidote to this is to slow your thinking and processing way down before you react. How does doing this work for you?

Your Takeaway: The next time you're in an intense situation, practice keeping your lips sealed in a long pregnant pause. By the time you count to 10, you may have an entirely different reaction than you would have had otherwise.

Exercise 6

Go back to the basics. Practice good self-care. Get seven to nine hours of sleep a night, drink plenty of water, eat healthy, exercise regularly, and schedule regular downtime for contemplation and reflection. How does this change daily life for you?

Your Takeaway: Keeping yourself healthy will help build your constitution so you can better adapt to stress.

Story Two: Steve

flexibility: the ability to adjust your emotions, thoughts and behavior to changing situations and conditions.
optimism: the ability to look at the brighter side of life and to maintain a positive attitude, even in the face of adversity (a focus on the future).

Flexibility is an important skill, because it allows us to roll with the punches and pivot quickly or adapt gracefully when a new direction is needed in our personal lives or the workplace. It encompasses resiliency and strength, which can help us adjust our emotions, thoughts and behavior to changing, unknown or unpredictable circumstances.

Flexible people are open-minded, and can change their position quickly they're presented with evidence that they're mistaken. Flexible people are agile and adapt quickly to new opportunities or ways of doing things when the landscape changes. Their ability to shift swiftly isn't indicative of their inability to commit to a direction; rather, it's the result of being able to tune into and digest constant feedback from their environment, while simultaneously keeping their footing.

When people aren't flexible, they're rigid and close-minded in their thinking. They're usually intolerant of different points of view, and don't take other perspectives or ways of doing things into account when making decisions. Instead, they give them short shrift. They're usually unable to react quickly enough to take advantage of new opportunities as they appear. They don't change their minds when presented with evidence that is contrary to their original position. They're fixed, rather than fluid.

It's important not to confuse assertiveness and flexibility. If you aren't openly considering valid suggestions from colleagues when you're faced with a problem, or you dismiss their suggestions without giving them a thought, you aren't being assertive. You're actually being inflexible and rigid.

No matter how long you've been in your current job or profession, it isn't possible for you to know everything or to predict future crises and developments by yourself. Technology's rapid pace has changed the way we do business, now at lightning speed. Years ago, no one would have predicted the Yellow Pages would become obsolete. To be a success today, it's important to listen to and weigh different suggestions and ideas to benefit from other perspectives. We all have our blind spots.

Optimism is the ability to see the positive attributes in negative circumstances. Optimistic people keep a bright attitude in the face of adversity. When I was a little girl, my father taught me to always search for the silver lining in any cloud. Psychologist Carl Jung wrote about a principle called the tension of the opposites, which is a common theory in many Eastern religions. It's the idea that any event or situation consists of two polar opposite extremes.

Think of the negative and positive poles or of a battery with two different charges. It's by experiencing the pressure of the two opposite poles that we eventually find our midpoint, or sweet spot. When something negative or unscripted occurs, an optimist sees the benefit in the hardship and values the lesson learned. In this way, she makes meaning out of suffering. Because of this perspective, she remains hopeful, bounces back and recovers more quickly from a setback than a pessimist.

One of the opposing forces that spoils optimism is negative thinking. When I was a little girl, I was riddled with anxiety and negative thoughts because I absorbed them from watching the adults around me. As a young adult, I worked very consciously, with help from a therapist, to defuse and reframe the negative self-talk into optimism. This change has greatly benefited me throughout my adult years. If I can do it and see benefit from it, so can you.

Being able to maintain a bright outlook and attitude, in addition to being able to access faith and hope, will help you stay unstuck and keep you moving in the face of hardship. Believing in the idea that if you take right action, or the next right step, you can work things out and resolve adversity, will help you execute in all aspects of life.

Early in my career, I had low optimism because I didn't like what I was doing. I had spent a lot of time gathering degrees and certifications, but going to work every day wasn't always fulfilling. To remedy the situation, I hired a career coach who helped me pinpoint my passion. One of the best exercises she assigned was for me to notice what I'd do all day in my free time, when I wasn't getting paid to do it. I spent my free time reading about psychology and talking to friends and family about their problems. I got really excited when people had aha moments.

Understanding myself and others, and what made people grow into their best selves, was my passion. Faith that we can change what we desire to reframe about ourselves was what got me out of bed in the morning. I was actually more optimistic than I had thought!

When I worked with my first clients, I couldn't believe I was being paid for it. I felt so much pleasure it felt like playing. Of course, being a coach requires a lot of hard work and training. What I'm suggesting though is that when a person works with passion, they're in their flow and hours can go by with minimal effort.

Steve's Story

Steve was trim and athletic – he carried 168 pounds on a 6'2" frame. He was into extreme sports, and especially liked mountain biking. He had thick, dark hair cut into the latest style, and dressed in the current hipster fashion. Steve was also smart: He had a degree in cybersecurity from the prestigious tech school MIT.

Steve came to see me because he wanted to learn to handle the stress he experienced at his job in cybersecurity at a large Fortune 500 healthcare organization. He did shift work, which meant working 12-hour days (and many nights) and part of the weekends, and often by himself – which is what he found most stressful. He defended against outside threats to the internal security of his company's information systems, a type of triage where he monitored the systems, deciding which threats needed to be investigated first and which could be passed to the day shift.

As he did this triage, he simultaneously investigated and worked on debugging potential threats. Steve, who was in his early 30s, was incredibly smart and knowledgeable about his work, taking it seriously and generally enjoying it. While his actual work didn't cause him stress, it was operating in isolation in 12-hour shifts for several days in a row that did it.

Plus, in his tech role, he worked behind a computer screen, rather than face-to-face with other people. When he returned home to sleep at dawn, everyone else was heading off to work. Steve didn't have many people to interact with during his awake downtimes. Since he enjoyed people and had a girlfriend and several close friends, this aspect of his work was very hard for him.

When Steve first contacted me, he was on temporary medical leave from his company and feared he was at the beginning stages of burnout. Doing technical work by himself for such a long stretch had him feeling down, and he needed time off to reflect, regroup and figure out what he wanted to do going forward. He wasn't certain he could handle this type of work and sleep schedule over the long haul, and was considering finding a different job.

The company he worked for was experiencing budget cuts because of a recent acquisition and merger with another large healthcare organization and was under an indefinite hiring freeze. Without the promise of the department hiring another worker to assist on the night shifts, he saw no relief in sight, which only compounded his feelings of stress.

The Evaluation

After Steve took the EQ-i 2.0 workplace assessment, and we debriefed his results, we learned he scored almost too high in social responsibility, average in self-regard, low in flexibility, and very low in stress tolerance and optimism. For these reasons, our worked focused on the Stress Management Composite.

Steve's goals for our work together were to lessen his periods of down feelings, and increase his satisfaction with his current circumstances at work. He also wanted to reduce his anxiety about his work and his future at the company. He wanted to increase his ability to deal with his present circumstances, which included not being able to see his friends and girlfriend as often as he'd like because of his schedule. Since the opportunities for normal, in-person communication with his relationships were limited, it made it harder for him to ascertain their true nature, especially when there were disagreements.

It's difficult to sort relationship issues out by e-mail or text only. Though it's not impossible, successful working-through requires expert communication skills from both parties. Steve felt increasing his ability to be flexible, handle stress better and become an expert communicator would elevate the overall quality of his daily life.

Steve didn't grow up in a family that was good at talking things out, nor did he learn communication skills while studying technology and computer science in graduate school. He described his parents as overly controlling, and said his extended family consisted mostly of Marines and engineers who were emotionally flat and big on having strict routines.

Since he described his grandmother as "liking things just so," I thought of the Stress Management Composite, and hypothesized that Steve was raised and influenced by people who most likely had a lack of flexibility.

I wondered how that impacted his own ability to manage stress. When I asked Steve this, he said he was indeed concerned about his own lack of flexibility. He thought it showed up in the fact that he had little work-life balance, although he attributed that mostly to his work schedule. After contemplating this for a moment, he indicated he was also worried about having a lack of social skills, since he didn't have anyone to talk to in person, either at work while working the night shifts or during the day when his friends were at work.

"My family is conservative and I'm not," he told me. Out of a need to let them know who he was and where he stood, he developed assertiveness skills early in life. This was a type of survival response so he could be himself amid a background of what he saw as emotional abuse. During most of his growing up years, his parents fought constantly, and often in front of Steve and his brothers. Steve played the role of shielding and protecting his siblings as much as possible from fights they shouldn't have heard.

There was one incident in particular that stood out his mind more than most. "My father took my siblings and me, and left the house with our suitcases packed," Steve said. "He drove cross-country and took us to his mother's house where we stayed for a month. However, this temporary separation didn't resolve my parents' fights. They continued the confrontations over the phone."

In addition, during that traumatic drive, Steve's father stopped along the way to where they were going and called his wife from a payphone. This altercation lasted several hours while Steve and his brothers sat in the car, in a strange state at an unfamiliar gas station. His father eventually returned home with the children, but it took years before their relationship would change for the better.

Steve and I talked about how experiences like this growing up prepared him to have independent thinking skills from an early age. By the time he physically became an adult, his parents told him they weren't ready to see him as an adult, and this was very difficult for him to understand. In actuality, he had been thinking and behaving like the most emotionally mature person in the household for many years.

His high independence combined with his high assertiveness skills allowed Steve to mature quickly, so much so that his contemporaries saw him as being intense and driven. In fact, Steve accomplished a lot at work and took his job very seriously. He had strong opinions about how things should be and how people should behave while working. This caused him to come across as more rigid and less flexible.

Steve admitted he overanalyzed situations to the point where he became numb and didn't know what his true emotions were anymore. This caused him to feel "uncalibrated," and he wanted to be in balance again.

"I want to learn to do some sort of proactive maintenance on myself and my emotions, so I won't feel like a robot anymore," he told me. "I want to feel more genuine and better balanced." He wanted to develop the capacity to be as adept at expressing his emotions as he already was with communicating his opinions and strong thoughts.

Steve's work life paralleled that of his family life: He felt a lot of pressure to perform at work and this was similar to the feelings of responsibility he felt in his family. In addition, the amount of stress he felt at work was similar to the tension he experienced at home when his parents were arguing. Since he had trouble asking for help in both places, despite his well-developed assertiveness skills, we agreed to work on developing the skill of asking for the support he needs. Too often, it was Steve's tendency to shoulder every burden by himself to the point where it drained and exhausted him. This is often the case when a person scores too high in social responsibility, and he puts other people's needs ahead of his own.

Like his parents, to some extent Steve was also very controlled and adept at suppressing unpleasant thoughts in the moment at the expense of them surfacing later. When he was alone, these repressed thoughts often came flying out in an overwhelming manner. "Negative thoughts come on quickly and suddenly, overtaking me and causing me a great deal of distress," he said, agreeing with me that it was time to change this pattern and get more skilled at asking for help.

The Work

Steve wanted to learn skills to cope with these situations, so I asked him to start journaling. He was excited about this and quickly found a technical smartphone app to help him journal in a way that was comfortable

– he called it Day One – and would help him be consistent. Since he felt he projected a rather stern persona when it came to standing up for himself (he reacted strongly any time he felt his boundaries were violated) and wanted to soften this, we started here first. He wanted to develop what he called "anchors" or tools to help him calm and soothe angry emotions when they were triggered.

Typically, when anxiety or angry emotions were triggered, he'd have what he called a "hijack" that lasted for an hour. He'd get caught up in his emotions and this would derail his ability to concentrate or be productive. We set a goal to shorten the duration of these upsets, decreasing them down to 45, 30, 15 and then zero minutes of quality time lost. To accomplish this, we had to build up his impulse control as well as his stress tolerance skills. Having this type of specific goal gave us a really solid benchmark to measure progress because it's easy to note and record time duration in a journal.

"It bothers me that I don't have a clear career path mapped out and have ambivalent feelings about whether or not I want to climb the ladder at my company," Steve told me.

Moreover, he wasn't sure he wanted to be a leader or manager of people because he felt so socially challenged when it came to relationships with colleagues. This was mostly because he considered himself a poor communicator.

Since I reassured Steve we could improve his communication skills with practice, I suggested we concentrate on helping him decide whether he wanted to stay at his company and whether he wanted to be promoted first.

At this point, Steve reiterated that he grew up in a family of Marines. He thought his direct and concise communication style was modeled and influenced by them. Since he worked the night shift, it forced most of his communications to be through e-mail, and he was concerned he came across poorly in this particular format.

One of the ways we approached this was for him to share some of his e-mails with me, and I helped him improve the language, tone and syntax of his messages. I was particularly conscious of helping him convey empathy and support in his conversations to foster better interpersonal relationships with his colleagues and members of other departments and teams.

He liked his approach and felt it was valuable in stretching his communication skills. One of the patterns he wanted to change and reformat was his tendency to withdraw from others and keep his emotions bottled up when stressed. He was learning this behavior wasn't healthy for him and was detrimental to his relationships with others. He realized it provoked angry emotions that didn't serve him well in the long run.

This behavior started to change when Steve got involved in a project at work that he was really passionate about: daily tracking of certain metrics to justify the addition of new employees. Steve enjoyed using his technology skills to figure out how to track the metrics and he was forced by his conviction to voice his opinion. He learned how to gather and use evidence to back up his opinion that additional staffers would help the department be more effective and productive, and that costs were certainly more than justified by the potential positive results. Steve was motivated to gather information and speak out because he felt he was going to bat for those he really cared about: his team members. In the end, this project was successful, which fueled the encouragement for Steve to continue.

After this project wrapped up and the department got approval to hire more people, Steve's boss said his performance was at the top of the team. He earned a raise and a fairly large bonus, as well as a special employee award that had to be approved by the executive committee. In addition, his boss told him she knew she could depend on him to get things done.

Since one of the upsets Steve had expressed to me in the beginning was a lack of feeling valued at work, this affirmation from his boss made a significant difference to him. He started to feel this company might actually be the right fit and stopped making plans to leave.

Steve had the additional insight that what was holding him back was a lack of access to information. To be secure and also perform at the top of his game, Steve desperately craved being at a level where he would be privy to knowing and understanding the direction the company was taking. He thought if he got one more promotion to a senior level, he'd have access to the level of influence he needed to be able to make a significant difference in the quality of life for the team. He took the opportunity of this occasion to explain to his boss that he wanted to be promoted and formally asked for her support. This was a significant improvement of his skills, because asking for help was challenging for him. Steve had to really want the change in order to push past his comfort zone, take the emotional risk and take action.

One specific action Steve took was to tell his boss he wanted to work days when the opportunity arose.

Although she supported him, in reality there wouldn't be an opportunity for some time. However, Steve was relieved to have an additional person on the night shift. Plus, he was improving his stress management skills. He was so good at growing these skills, that by the time the opportunity arose to work days, he wondered if he still wanted to make that change. He had to rethink it, but eventually took the option to switch.

When I asked Steve to list his strengths, he identified he was good at cross-team relationship building relationships with people outside his team. His friends confirmed this by telling him they saw him as a warm, supportive and easy person to open up to and talk with although he was mystified by this description of himself: This was an aspect of his personality he didn't focus on very much. "Maybe I'm more suited to a corporate career than I originally gave myself credit for," he told me. Now that he felt valued, Steve accessed his self-actualization skills, and realized he wanted to stay and see how far he could rise within the organization.

His internal motivation was to see how much influence he could garner to effect systemic change that could benefit his entire team. He wanted to find a way to increase the team's productivity and efficiency while at the same time increasing their sense of work-life balance. He remembered that when he was in college he was involved in student leadership and had access to communication training. One of the training topics covered was called unconscious bias and it dealt with unravelling preconceived notions or biases people have, a topic that really resonated with him.

Our discussion about this realization planted the seeds for him to see himself more authentically. While he used to believe he was a poor communicator, he was learning it wasn't actually true. Although it was true that he grew up in a family of non-communicators, he wasn't totally like them. In fact, he was a good communicator and was interested in learning even more about communication to further enhance his skills. Adjusting his own perception of himself to fit reality empowered Steve to further take charge of his life and career.

At this point in our work, I focused on helping Steve learn to recognize the advance warning signs that signaled when he was becoming over-extended and emotionally fatigued. Since he cared so much about others' well-being, one of the things he had to learn was how to balance meeting his own emotional needs with helping his friends and coworkers meet theirs. He was beginning to understand he couldn't put the needs of other people ahead of his own, without taking care of himself, because this wasn't sustainable over the long term.

"I've never noticed the negative psychological affects created by over-extending myself until now," Steve told me. Like a lightbulb going on in his head, he put two and two together and made a decision to shift focus to bringing this into balance. He used his time with me and writing in his journal to raise his consciousness about this issue and improve his stress tolerance. In addition, we worked on increasing his self-regard so it would be in balance with his social responsibility. These are the two skills which must be in balance so people don't over-give to others, including their employer or other groups and organizations, at their own expense or detriment.

The Results

As a result of our work together, Steve told me he was finding relief and was less frustrated with his work and himself. He was learning to distinguish the voice of reason from the voices of anxiety and rumination, and by doing so he was taking charge and getting his life back on track. He was more fulfilled at work because he had become better at voicing his opinion via assertiveness and asking for what he needed. For example, one of the things he requested was to be a teaching resource or tutor for onboarding new employees. He'd been a teaching assistant in graduate school and recently identified that he missed using this skill.

In addition, he was very confident about his ability to be a good teacher and always received positive feedback that he was good at it. This was what encouraged him to ask for this new task and he was pleased his boss took him up on it. He found a lot of pleasure in training the new department hires and with his new relationship skills he quickly helped them assimilate into the team. He reflected that at the beginning of his job he felt a fair amount of imposter syndrome, which he said was "soul sucking," but now he felt really competent at work with his team. In fact, his team had become a second family to him.

Because he felt part of this pseudo-family, he relaxed and became more flexible and comfortable at work. This also helped him with his stress tolerance and coping skills, because he trusted himself, his boss and team members to have his back; he knew he could ask for what he needed when he required more support. He also had improved clarity, vision and sense of purpose. He was in the process of mapping out his career, which was one of his initial goals, and was assigned an internal mentor, a male senior executive, to help him rise up the ranks. With so much promise for the future, Steve felt relaxed, comfortable, competent and validated.

Building Your Flexibility and Optimism

Today, we have the opportunity to benefit from the latest and greatest research from neurobiologists and their study of our brains. While a few decades ago it may have sounded like New Age woo-woo to talk about the power of positive thinking, today neuroscientists can study MRIs and tell us how negative and positive thinking stresses or benefits the brain.

One of their findings that's relevant to optimism is the maximum that neurons that fire together wire together. This means that if you're thinking negatively (or positively), it becomes a habit pattern in your brain's neural pathways and networks. Since you can just as easily choose positive thinking over negative thinking, and that choice has so many healthy brain benefits, why wouldn't you?

If you still have irrational thoughts from childhood (and most of us do), and have already formed negative habit patterns, it takes effort to change and rewire the brain. Consistency is key, and regular daily practice is best, even if you only have five minutes.

Neurobiologists are also studying neuroplasticity, which refers to the brain's ability to change throughout a person's lifetime. The human brain has the ability to reorganize itself by developing new connections between brain cells, called neurons. Neuroplasticity refers to the change in neural pathways and synapses that occurs in response to certain behaviors, environments or neural processes. When these changes occur, the brain performs synaptic pruning and deletes neural connections that are no longer necessary, in addition to strengthening the ones needed the most.

This is amazing and hopeful news when it comes to the ability to be flexible.

When we're stuck in a negative rut or thought pattern, with effort and attention, we can consciously grow a new neural pathway that's more beneficial. I recently attended a workshop called "The Neurobiology of Addiction," held at Maryville University of St. Louis and presented by Christopher La Tourette La Riche, M.D. In his lecture, Dr. La Riche stated that longevity and quality of life improve when we continue to stretch past our comfort zones and learn new behaviors.

This can be as simple as trying a new food or restaurant, or traveling to see a new place. It can also be as complicated as earning a new university degree. Keeping our brains nimble and flexible helps us adapt to our lives' changing course as well as enables us to appreciate another person's point of view.

Taking the time to learn to be flexible will help you be more adaptable as well as have a higher quality of life. It can even help you live longer.

Exercises for Exploration and Mastery: Flexibility and Optimism

Try these exercises to work on your flexibility and optimism skills.

Exercise 1

Consider optimism vs. pessimism. Think of someone you know (either at work, home or in the public eye) who's a positive thinker. Make a list of their attributes: anything you can define that classifies them as seeing things with a bright attitude. Once your list is complete, compare yourself to see how you measure up. How many things do you have in common with them? Are there any characteristics on the list that you'd like to cultivate? If there are, make a plan to spend time focusing on developing these qualities daily.

Your Takeaway: Repeat the same exercise with someone you know who's a negative thinker, and identify the attributes you'd like to extinguish in your own behavior.

Exercise 2

Think about "The Sunny Side of the Street." Listen to the song (or read the lyrics) to "The Sunny Side of the Street" by Louis Armstrong. Even though the musician probably didn't study neuroscience, the lyrics seem to convey that he knew we could redirect our consciousness at will. Here's an excerpt: "Leave your worries on the doorstep, just direct your feet to the sunny side of the street ...I used to walk in the shade, with those blues on parade, but I'm not afraid, baby ... with gold dust at my feet, on the sunny side of the street." You can use these words to cheer yourself, or you can find another positive song that helps shift your mood when necessary. How do you feel when you do this?

Your Takeaway: Happy, inspirational music is uplifting even without lyrics, and access to such music is easier now than ever before.

Exercise 3

Listen to audiobooks or podcasts to set a positive mood. First thing in the morning, after I complete my exercise, I script a positive mood by listening to the ideas of people who inspire me to see things from a higher perspective. Listening to motivational podcasts helps me start the day in a positive frame of mind. I see it as nourishment: food for the brain and support for the soul. Whenever possible, I repeat this at lunchtime. Where could you fit this practice into your day?

Your Takeaway: Do some research and experiment to find out what type of reading or listening motivates you and sets you on a positive course.

Exercise 4

Practice listening to other points of view. Intentionally seek out a coworker, family member or friend who you know has a point of view that's different from your own. Interview her or simply ask questions, while keeping a curious tone in your voice. Listen to her with focused attention and be sincerely interested in her perspective. Take care not to criticize or debate her point of view. Just listen. What can you learn from them? How might listening to their point of view cause you to make changes to your own?

Your Takeaway: Every client I work with has a different point of view. I practice listening to all of them, non-judgmentally, while using my body language to convey genuine interest. I'm naturally curious about how other people see the world, as I feel it enriches my own worldview. What about you? Can you communicate a curious and non-judgmental stance while you listen?

Exercise 5

Surrender control. This is an exercise I often assign to couples who seek me out because they've lost their spark. Esther Perel is a Belgian psychotherapist who's well-known for her research on the human tension between the need for security and the need for adventure. Her research suggests that when we become too comfortable in our set routines, they become lifeless and possibly boring, too. To put some excitement back into your daily life, her research suggests trying something new and including an element of surprise.

Does this sound familiar? It reminds me of the research on neuro-plasticity and changing or growing the healthy brain. You don't have to be a couple to do this exercise. The next time you're going somewhere with another person (it could be a coworker, boss, friend or client), ask him to select the venue or activity and say "yes" to whatever he chooses. If you're trying this with your significant other (or someone you know fairly well and trust implicitly), you might be adventurous and ask him to keep the venue or experience a secret and surprise you at the last minute.

Your Takeaway: Most clients, albeit skeptical at first, have told me this is one of their favorite exercises because they end up doing things they never would have done on their own, at least without a nudge.

Exercise 6

Ask for feedback. During the next week, when you catch yourself behaving inflexibly, circle back and ask the people you were interacting with what they noticed about your behavior. Did they think you were rigid and closed off to their ideas? Is there something they'd like to see you change about yourself? Take in their information, write it down, and think about it.

Your Takeaway: Use your reality testing skill to discern whether their perspective is accurate and whether you need to make the changes they suggest.

Exercise 7

Notice the contrast between flexibility, assertiveness, inflexibility and unassertiveness. Review your behavior this week and ask yourself if you were being assertive or truly inflexible. Remember that assertiveness is the ability to stand up for yourself, voice your opinion and be able to negotiate a win-win situation. By contrast, when you're inflexible, you're defending your stance despite valid and rational evidence to the contrary. If you're too accommodating to other people's agendas, then you're being unassertive.

Your Takeaway: Attempt to identify behavior that is assertive and flexible vs. unassertive and inflexible.

Case Study

Tying It All Together: Happiness, the Well-Being Indicator

> **happiness**: the ability to feel satisfied with your life, to enjoy yourself and others, and to have fun (a focus on the present).

In the EQ-i 2.0 model, happiness, or well-being, contributes to and is a result of emotional intelligence. This 16th skill is a barometer for a person's general emotional health and overall good functioning. The four subscales most closely associated with happiness are self-regard, self-actualization, interpersonal relationships and optimism.

Self-regard is related because happiness is a byproduct of believing and trusting in yourself, and living life in integrity according to your own value system. Strengthening self-regard helps improve a person's general satisfaction with life.

Self-actualization is also a factor because happiness is the result of a willingness to learn and grow, and live in a self-directed way. Happy people are motivated from within, and commit to developing their passions in life, which leads to a richer, more-enhanced quality of life.

Interpersonal relationships are involved because happy people develop emotionally supportive alliances that act as a buffer to life's ups and downs. No person is an island, and people who are emotionally intimate with others live healthier, longer and more fulfilling lives.

Optimism is related because people who are more resilient in the face of setbacks don't allow themselves to shrink into depression or disappointment when things don't go as planned. Optimistic people have the ability to see the best in a situation, and they keep moving forward, which of course makes them happier.

By contrast, a person who has a low degree of this emotional intelligence component may suffer from symptoms of depression, anxiety or worry, self-destructive thoughts, or withdrawal from friends, family, and coworkers. This behavior isn't life-affirming, and most people in this state of mind report feeling down or sad most of the time.

Happiness is an inside job, and according to research, it isn't highly correlated with material well-being. *The EQ Edge: Emotional Intelligence and Your Success* by Steven J. Stein, Ph.D. and Howard E. Book, M.D. cites research showing that in the United States, billionaires report being only slightly happier than people with average incomes.

Plus, even though personal income has more than doubled between 1960 and the late 1990s, the portion of people who report being happy has remained stable at 30%. The research also indicated that once you're above the poverty line, additional money contributes little difference to your happiness. Components such as self-esteem, a sense of personal control, extroversion and optimism matter much more.

Amy fell in this category of people who had high achievement and material wealth, but remained dissatisfied and unhappy with her life. Amy was overweight. At 5'8", she was 180 pounds. Born in Wisconsin and raised on a farm, she was used to hard work and high achievement. In fact, she won the 4-H prize for her community service project five years in a row at the Wisconsin state fair. A graduate of Marquette University, she had a keen interest in quilting as a hobby. With dark brown hair and brown eyes, she was a human dynamo and a true force to be reckoned with.

Introduction and Presenting Issues

The CEO of a financial services firm referred her employee, 35-year-old Amy, to me because Amy's behavior was disrupting the team. She was impulsive and would intrusively burst into her boss's office to spend an hour or two venting and complaining. Although Amy was a top producer at her financial services firm and was successful, she was anxious and unhappy, scoring in the low range for well-being.

Remember, Dr. Reuven Bar-On's research focused on answering two questions: What makes people successful and what makes them happy? Both are necessary for a high emotional intelligence score. A lower happiness score may easily dampen the overall stellar effects of high scores in other subscales. For example, if you score low in happiness, you may find it difficult to influence or inspire others, or view life as all work and no play. You may even withdraw from leadership responsibilities, colleagues, social situations and friends.

Although it's not considered a subscale in one of the five composites, well-being or happiness is the 16th skill in Dr. Bar-On's model. In part, the emotional intelligence score takes four other skills into account when calculating a metric: self-regard, interpersonal relationships, self-actualization and optimism.

Amy was especially competitive with her peers. Sadly, she told me during our work together that she valued herself primarily by her monthly production numbers, which then determined her income. When her monthly production was high, she felt very good about herself and when it was low her anxiety ate at her self-regard. From that vantage point, the whole world looked dull and gloomy to her. She felt lost, and she lacked clarity and the ability to roll with the ups and downs of her chosen profession.

Not only was Amy miserable during these periods but she made everyone else around her unhappy, too. She was moody and irritable, which had a negative effect on her relationships with family, coworkers and staff members. She shut down and closed herself off from opportunities and possibilities. In addition, she was quickly triggered and acted impulsively. When angry, she sometimes slammed drawers, yelled and swiped things off her desk in one quick arm motion, causing everything in sight to fall on the floor in tangled-up chaos. When she was anxious, she also spent precious time developing new strategies to feel successful again.

While Amy acknowledged how her lack of optimism, stress tolerance and impulse control negatively controlled her, she has no idea how to change these behaviors. Needless to say she was a very intense, driven person. Her mind frequently raced – her ideas colliding with each other, and she talked incessantly and very fast. I needed double my usual concentration skills to listen to and follow the disparate threads of her conversation. At the end of each meeting I was exhausted because of the energy required to understand what she wanted to convey to me. I surmised her colleagues and clients must experience the same thing as me.

I had to increase my own self-regard and assertiveness skills because I often felt Amy didn't value the work we were doing. On one hand, she'd tell me she had plenty of money and could purchase what she wanted without negative consequences; on the other, I got the distinct impression she didn't like paying my fee. She often said I was charging too much or taking advantage of her. Her behavior hooked my own fears of not providing enough value, so I under-promised and over-delivered, and I failed to charge for all my time.

Listening to her complain about my fee each time we met was tedious, yet informative, for me. I realized this was a projection of what Amy was experiencing internally – tedium and strained effort. At the same time, I realized the situation wasn't healthy for me, and my conscious awareness was a valuable lesson for me. Amy's fears and projections were a gift for me because I learned to step up my own self-regard in relation to my work.

In addition, Amy had a very strong personality, dominating our discussions even though she asked me to stop her when she stepped into that behavior. When I interrupted her, even though she had requested it, she ignored me and continued speaking. This cycle continued for a number of months. I was constantly on my toes, with my assertiveness turned up to full volume.

The Initial Consult

When first meeting a client, I usually deliver the EQ-i 2.0 assessment report results and debrief him or her. This was my intention with Amy, but the initial consult didn't go as planned. When I arrived, she appeared prepared to go over the report results because I saw them on her computer monitor. Instead, she wanted to share a lot about her personal life and her work.

She seemed stressed, speaking quickly, with a sense of urgency, as if she felt pressured to fit everything into one meeting. I felt the fire-hose effect, being blasted with an overload of information. There was no space between Amy's words for me to even comment on what she told me.

Wanting to be respectful of her needs, I didn't interrupt her. We didn't review Amy's assessment results or cover expectations and goals for our meetings. At the time, though I was uncomfortable with this approach, I saw no harm in waiting until our second meeting to return to the original agenda. In hindsight, I later saw this first meeting as a huge tell. It was a microcosm of how Amy typically conducted her life, a freeze frame of the structure of what was to come.

A better approach would have been to take a firmer stance at that first meeting. My desire to make Amy feel comfortable, coming from my own high scores in empathy and interpersonal relationships, set the stage for this continuing pattern of relating. During subsequent meetings, it became even more difficult for me to interrupt and stop the fire hose of flooding information.

While Amy indicated her personal life was extremely stressful, she made it clear to me that discussions about it were off-limits. This was a major concern to me because we'd be eliminating and ignoring an area that had limitless potential for moving Amy's work objectives forward. I agreed to accommodate her wishes, but I explained we'd need to revisit this issue in the future. I was certain the stress at home was robbing her of the energy and creativity she needed at work to fulfill her goals.

My professional experience tells me people can't operate indefinitely on the basis of being one person at home and another at work. Perhaps we can carry this off for a while, but inevitably it becomes too burdensome and we collapse from the stress. We're seamless personalities, and whether at work or at home, we need to behave in an integrated way that allows us to reach our full potential.

Though it took some time, Amy outlined goals for our work together during our first meeting:

- to be authentic and to follow her own path to success

- to figure out who she is so she can approach work in her own unique manner, without having to emulate others' approaches

- to win at work, knowing she does a really good job

- to have no regrets

- to comfortably set expectations when working with her clients

- to know when she has influence with others

- to position herself as an expert in her field

- to identify her target market and ideal client profile.

With all this in mind, I used Dr. Bar-On's EQ model to map out Amy's status quo and the skills we needed to work on to bring her emotional intelligence up to a level that would allow her to achieve her desired results:

- Amy scored low on emotional self-awareness and empathy, which explained her lack of ability to discern when she was influencing someone and when she wasn't. Successful leaders understand themselves and their own emotions before they can express empathy for those they lead to be perceived as relatable. Amy didn't have the ability to accurately recognize and understand her own feelings.

- She scored low in flexibility, which suggested she tended to stick to tried-and-true methods in her leadership approach and the goals she set with her team. This was a likely source for her lack of inspiration when it came to innovation and progress. Sticking to the tried-and-true methods limited her ability to think creatively and outside the box, which explained why she struggled to find and implement her own unique approach.

- She scored low in reality testing, which explained why she struggled to convey her expectations to her clients, who might view her expectations as very high, unrealistic or even unattainable. She needed to tune into her clients' current life state to be seen as trustworthy and inspirational to have influence with them.

- Amy scored very high on assertiveness, almost to the point of being aggressive, so she didn't have a problem communicating her thoughts or opinions with others. If a different client had this issue I may have suggested we work on building assertiveness skills, but in this case, I suggested she tone it down.

- Amy scored low in emotional expression and this affected her ability to share a compelling vision with her team. She was too ready to express negative emotions such as irritability, anxiety and anger. She didn't have the proficiency to express a full range of emotions, both positive and negative, affecting her ability to be authentic and genuine.

- She scored high in independence and that could have been why she needed to do things her own way. Her score was so high we considered whether she had a tendency to leave others behind.

- Amy scored high in self-actualization; that explained her need to be sure she was doing the best job she possibly could, achieving winning results.

Here's a summary of our developmental plan:

- **Self-regard**: Amy scored average in self-regard so I suggested we work on strengthening this skill first, as many of the others build on this one, most notably emotional self-awareness and empathy. If she wasn't secure in herself, she probably had trouble tolerating and accepting constructive feedback.

- After working on self-regard, I suggested building **emotional self-awareness**. Some of Amy's life experiences had left her with a sense of shame and guilt, though she avoided discussing this with me at first. We needed to clear the shame and undo the guilt to make room for healthy self-acceptance and self-compassion. Once we accomplished this, there would be room for greater self-understanding and self-worth, which in turn would make it easier for Amy to be emotionally understanding with others.

- **Empathy**, or the ability to understand and appreciate other people's feelings and points of view, is the most important skill for resonant leaders today. It was imperative for Amy to develop this skill so she could connect emotionally and build trust with clients, coworkers, staff and family members.

- **Flexibility**: Because Amy had average self-regard and low flexibility, she wasn't very coachable. Although she wanted new ideas from me, it was hard for her to hear them even when I delivered them carefully. She had set habits and fixed ideas, and even though she acknowledged they weren't working for her, she was reluctant to make any changes. Her limited flexibility kept her stuck. My intention was to help her create a greater range of flexibility by encouraging her to take very small steps in new directions to loosen her perceptions.

- **Reality testing**: I suggested Amy work on her ability to assess the correspondence between what she experiences and what objectively exists without letting emotions cloud her perspective. My goal was to help her achieve more clarity, which I believed would also increase her sense of security, lower her anxiety and strengthen her self-regard. If she could learn to judge her self-worth by factors other than her monthly production results, she'd have a more balanced outlook on life. Instead of the emotional instability that was common for her, I hoped she could develop a more consistent and optimistic attitude.

Second Consult

In my experience, clients achieve their goals more effectively when they agree to meet weekly. If a client can't do that, meeting biweekly is second best. I only have a handful of clients who see me monthly, and while some do achieve their goals this way, our work isn't as effective or fulfilling as it could be. A month went by before Amy agreed to meet again, which was acceptable, but not optimal.

Here's what I planned to cover in the second meeting: my client paperwork and the expectations I had for Amy; any questions she might have for me; her reactions to our first meeting; her EQ-i 2.0 results; and creating her developmental plan.

During this second meeting, Amy was adamant that she wanted me to tell her what to do - where and what to focus on, and in what order. She had a strong need for structure and asked me to treat her like she treated her clients when making financial suggestions to them. Her request intrigued me.

When I work with clients, I accommodate their unique, individual learning styles as much as possible. Although there are similar threads and themes that run through every case, such as the EQ model itself and the 16 skills, it's impossible to predict how things will go and to know in advance what's in someone's best interests. I prefer to allow the situation to unfold and evolve rather than attempt to force the process to a preconceived conclusion.

"If I tell you what to do, you'll be dependent on me forever to give you a sense of direction," I told her, explaining that the intent behind our work was to help her develop her own dependable inner compass that would guide her to her appropriate actions and wise decisions. "Developing this inner guidance system takes time to cultivate, and there's no way to predict how long it'll take," I said.

To help others develop their instincts and intuition, I typically ask a lot of questions that make them dive deep inside themselves so they know when they've hit pay dirt, when they've had an aha moment.

It was during this second meeting with Amy that I also discussed the idea of crafting a professional communications statement she could use with her clients to set the tone for their work together. In response, she shared examples of things she had said in the past to clients, and her statements seemed disjointed and potentially confusing to a prospect. This was because Amy had conflict around money, including fears of being taken advantage of by clients, service providers and her management company.

She behaved with her prospects and clients the same way she did with me. The dynamic that caused her to question whether she was getting equivalent value for what she paid out was occurring at a meta-level with her clients and was obvious to them. In one form or another, her message to her potential clients was, "I'm not here to take advantage of you, but I won't help you unless I get compensated. I won't give advice away for free."

That meant Amy didn't have a "give before you receive" mindset. Because she was almost paranoid that clients would take advantage of her time and skills, she was hesitant to offer any free advice or suggestions without first making sure she'd be paid. This was partly why she failed to build relationships of trust and respect with prospective clients on any consistent basis.

Like many other financial services professionals, Amy suffered from chronic anxiety over not knowing from where the next deal was coming. This anxiety weighed her down and affected her moods. "I feel a lack of control over accomplishing my business goals," she told me.

For homework, I asked Amy to write down her client approach language and to reflect on times when those words had landed well and when they had distanced the client. I asked her to put herself in her prospects' shoes and attempt to imagine what they'd need to hear while at the same time communicating what she wanted to convey.

"A successful relationship involves mutuality, reciprocity, trust and respect," I explained. "Imagine statements that would embody these principles."

I suggested she be prepared to practice these statements with me the next time we met and I'd role play being the client until she was comfortable with the new language.

To address some of her anxiety, I suggested Amy sit with her feelings of uncertainty and attempt to understand them. Sitting in the "not knowing" and embracing it would be the process to finding her own creativity. This process would help her discover her own unique way of prospecting that would, over time, produce consistent results. I suspected Amy would also experience less anxiety once she was clear about her unique method.

Third Consult

After our initial meeting, I suggested to Amy that it would be more effective to limit our discussions one concern at a time. This proved difficult for her, perhaps because her brain was often racing in different directions at once. During each meeting, I struggled to control the fire-hose effect because Amy always presented too much information to cover realistically during our appointments. During this consult, she asked for more time, so we spent two hours together. I suggested we meet in the future for 90 minutes instead of 50, but she declined.

Although we had planned to discuss her approach language, Amy had high anxiety and a sense of urgency about other topics so I deferred to her. "I'm mostly concerned that although my income has been tracking on course for the year I feel like I wasn't performing as well as I could have been," she told me. "I want to know why I'm not happy even though I've just had my best production year ever."

Amy was also concerned she wasn't leading her team to produce to the best of their ability. She wanted to know what was holding her back from being a better leader and wanted to take a step back to allow her staff to step forward and manage themselves in her absence.

She spoke to me at length about her lack of ability to handle adversity and how she was challenged to maintain control in the face of emotional upset. She recognized that when she was emotionally triggered at work, she often became irritable and expressed her negativity by slamming drawers and pounding on her desk. Although she originally said she didn't want to discuss her personal life, she talked about the negative affects her behavior had on her family.

She saw a connection between the negative way her parents behaved when she was growing up and the way she was behaving now. I told Amy I wanted to dig in and understand more about the messages she received from her parents while growing up. I explained these messages would have formed neurological templates that we could work together to reframe and redirect in a more positive way.

Amy was genuinely distressed about this revelation and I was touched by her sincere need to make changes in her behavior. These confessions brought out my own desire to help her face her unresolved emotional issues and grow from them. I told her that her sincerity elicited great empathy and compassion in me so she could start to understand the reciprocal nature of trusted relationships. "I want to help you find joy, balance and peace, in addition to the great passion you already have for your work," I told her. "As you develop patience, also called impulse control, you'll get there."

"No matter what I do, though, I'm never happy," Amy said, which confirmed that her low score in the well-being/happiness indicator was accurate. She was emphatic about how important it was that she be more at peace, better at communicating and reach her true potential, explaining her high self-actualization score.

In this same discussion, Amy said she wanted better results when working with female prospects and clients. Often when she had a meeting scheduled with, for example, a married couple, the female client didn't come to the appointment. "I want to understand why this happens and what I can do to prevent it," she said. I suggested she build her empathy and learn to be more relational with women so they'd feel heard. This would encourage them to interact more collaboratively with her.

"How can I learn to be authentic, and to understand what it means to have an authentic brand?" Amy said.

"The more you know and understand yourself, the easier it'll be for you to present your brand authentically," I told her.

At this point in the conversation, I suggested we turn our attention to some exercises for building self-regard. We didn't finish all of the exercises I had in mind, so I assigned them for homework, offering more exercises than usual after this consult. The homework addressed the plethora of ideas we had discussed, corralling the various topics into something manageable to examine at our next meeting.

Here are the exercises I suggested for Amy's homework:

1. Since you want to reach your full potential, write out: What does full potential really mean? How will you recognize it when you get there? Will you know it when you see it? What will be different about your life when you arrive there? How will you benchmark your progress toward this goal?

2. Identify the benefits of increasing your self-regard and how they'll affect yourself, your organization and your family. Brainstorm ways to work on a more positive attitude and write them down. Here are ideas to get you started: Write down three things you're grateful for at the end of each day. Listen to a podcast or recording that's inspirational or motivational every morning either when you're working out, showering or driving to work. Or, make up your own affirmations and start using them daily. Decide how

much time you can spend in quiet daily reflection or contemplation, and commit to this appointment with yourself. This is a primary means to building self-regard, the foundation for reaching
other skills goals.

3. If one of your barriers to self-regard is the need to improve your
communication skills with clients and your team, specifically
about what they can expect from you and what you can expect
from them, select a client or team member with whom you can
practice your communication skills. Start by simply asking them
how they're doing. Do they have questions? Do they understand
your expectations of them? Is there anything they'd like you to
do? Is there anything they'd like you to communicate differently?

4. List your strengths, such as loyalty, sense of humor, hard work,
honesty and so on. Review these daily for affirmation and inspiration.

5. Practice this affirmation out loud in front of the mirror daily: "I'm
no longer working with people who don't value my expertise.
From now on I'm working with high net-worth professionals and
ideal clients. I trust myself to do my best work. I'm now available
to receive only the best clients. Let those who need me find me.
Let me help them truly build their highest net worth."

6. As you try to find your path, you often bounce between one extreme and the other, or employ rigid, black-and-white thinking.
Brainstorm ways you could land in the middle and find your gray
zone.

Fourth Consult

Amy began our appointment by letting me know she was excited after
our last meeting and felt I was helping her move forward on her goals.
She also said that while she valued our meetings, she didn't like paying
my fee. Then, for the rest of her check-in time, Amy talked about having
the gut feeling that she had reached peak production performance and
wouldn't be able to rise any higher in her organization.

"I believe the problems I'm experiencing are typical of those that
others at my level face," she said. "I'm anxious because I believe I'm
facing issues that are endemic to my industry, so it's out of my control."

Amy also had problems training her staff. They interrupted her with technical questions and this broke her concentration, triggering her irritability so she didn't know how to manage them. I offered to interview her staff and also do a 360-degree review to ascertain where the bottleneck was occurring. This exercise would offer the added bonus of uncovering whether her staff viewed her as authentic or not, which Amy said was a top priority.

When we were going over her homework from the previous meeting, Amy said acquiring new clients was her biggest challenge. She wanted the new clients to be high net-worth individuals but she didn't meet enough of these prospects. This discussion triggered her anxiety and she expressed the desire to invent her own referral system again, which in turn sparked another discussion about whether or not she could reach her full potential.

This discussion was a good example of how scoring high in self-actualization without being balanced in other emotional intelligence areas isn't necessarily beneficial. Amy scored high in self-actualization and lower in interpersonal relationship skills. When these two components are more balanced, a person invests time and effort into pursuing his or her own personal goals, while at the same time fostering meaningful relationships with others.

Although developing interpersonal relationships has many benefits, Amy had trouble asking people for help because she was so independent. I attempted to help her see that significant people in her life could play an integral role in helping her reach goals that she might not be able to achieve on her own. This is why I had encouraged her to spend more time developing personal relationships with her staff and key people on her team. "I wonder how I could be as good at establishing personal rapport as I am at doing the technical aspects of my job," she said.

For homework after this meeting, I asked Amy to keep a journal and start recording any anxious thoughts she had on a daily basis so I could get a better understanding of how often she had them and how they affected her. I wanted to identify and understand her triggers and patterns even further.

Fifth Consult

We began this meeting reviewing the anxieties that Amy had noted in her journal. Here are some that we reviewed:

- Amy was anxious about where new prospects and clients would come from, pinpointing this as a constant source of her stress. I pointed out that while some of this stress was valid, I hypothesized some of it was due to her emotional reaction to overwhelm. I suggested she do research to find out how her peers were obtaining prospects and clients, and then do strategic planning to map out the actions she could take to find her ideal clients. We'd then couple this with a combination of mindfulness techniques to manage and combat the stress.

- She was anxious about making sure she had a full appointment schedule. I suggested working on the business is just as important as working in the business; plus, revenue-generating activities need to be balanced with strategic-planning activities. In fact, when this balance is achieved, most people experience less emotional stress.

- Amy was worried that if she didn't worry about work, things wouldn't work out. I told her just the opposite is true. When the conscious mind is relaxed, the unconscious mind opens and delivers the perfect solution, an experience of being "in the flow." That's the reason why it's so important to relax and be mindful. Other antidotes to anxiety include gathering information and taking action. Doing research, whether on how to prospect or how to grow the business, is a positive step toward moving forward and directly combating worry. Thinking strategically and planning ahead is another way.

- Amy considered herself a hunter, yet felt the hunting was getting stressful. I suggested she become less of a hunter and more of a receiver. I talked to her about developing an abundance mindset instead of a scarcity mindset. It's more comfortable to attract business through referrals than to hunt down new clients. Building her empathy and using it to connect with people emotionally would enable her to become better at receiving referrals. Most people like to help those who are genuine and have done a good job for them. Then we talked about how independent she was and how that worked against developing her empathy. She traced her strong independent behavior to circumstances that existed while growing up with her father. Empathy is a skill that can be learned and as long Amy was patient, or had impulse control, she could develop it. I gave her permission to practice with me.

- She said she was competitive and had a hard time letting things go when she didn't win at getting new business, closing a new deal, or winning first place at the company golf tournament, for example. I suggested we work on her ability to accept what actually is and detach from emotional reactions to less-than-expected results.

I gave Amy homework that would help develop her reality testing and suggested she write the following statements in her journal on a daily basis: "I observe people and situations objectively and fairly. I value the composite of my qualities and characteristics. I communicate what I see in such an objective and integral way that it can be received and heard. I deeply honor and value the unlimited resource of creativity that's within me that I'm free to express in both family and career situations."

Sixth Consult

During our sixth consult, Amy seemed more relaxed, open to my suggestions, authentic and fully present. Her mind didn't seem to be racing as much. She focused on fewer topics and we were able to take a deeper dive into what she presented for the day. She started our meeting by sharing two different examples of how people made requests for charitable giving and wanted to compare them to how she wanted to treat her clients.

The first example was when a former boss told her she owed it to the profession to contribute to a certain charity, and the second was when a nonprofit organization hosted a tour of its facility and explained how her donation would be used to help their clients.

Amy told me the second way was the style she preferred to embrace when she was explaining her process and how she worked to her clients and prospects. I suggested this realization offered a great deal of insight into how to engage and motivate people as well as how to talk to her ideal clients. Her preferred method was called pull marketing or following the law of attraction (that's prosperity thinking) instead of push marketing, which is old school and fear-based (that's scarcity thinking). As she could tell from her own experience, pull marketing is not only more palatable, but is based on interpersonal relationships and works better in today's market

As my friend Meridith Elliott Powell explains in her book, *Winning in the Trust and Value Economy: A Guide to Sales Success and Business Growth*, the new economy is one in which consumers have many buying choices so they won't tolerate old school and aggressive selling techniques. Instead, today's buyer purchases based on the trust and value they have in relation to their service provider. If that relationship becomes tarnished, they move on to buy from someone else because it's easy to find another vendor.

I discussed with Amy how the forward-thinking charity in her example was successful because it offered her a personal experience of how her donation would be effectively used, and she got to see those benefits firsthand. This was the precise information that allowed her to articulate the value of her services to her own clients. I saw she was making progress on developing empathy, being able to put herself in someone else's shoes and see things from their point of view, and I was excited for her.

Seventh Consult

As we started this meeting, Amy said, "I want to focus on maximizing my potential. How can I start doing this?" This question again reflected her high score in self-actualization and the lack of balance between that and her low scores in other emotional intelligence skills that tended make her hyper-focused on this one area.

Sometimes scoring high in one subscale, when not balanced by another, can hinder one's success. Clearly in Amy's case, she repeatedly came back to focus on this one skill she was comfortable with, to the detriment of other skills. People like Amy who score high in self-actualization may be less tolerant of those who aren't continuously trying to improve or may come across as know-it-alls. They also may be prone to take on too much and then suffer burnout, plus they're often viewed as workaholics. It can be helpful to ask such individuals how they define work-life balance and how their choices impact those around them, both at home and work.

I reminded Amy she had scored inside the Leadership Gold Bar for self-actualization on the assessment where the top 50% of leaders score, which explained why she had such a strong desire to improve herself and pursue meaningful objectives. For comparative purposes, I offered her two career profiles from *The EQ Edge: Emotional Intelligence and Your*

Success with research data on the top five skills needed for success in her field:

- **Insurance sales**: assertiveness, self-regard, happiness, stress tolerance and self-actualization

- **Financial services professionals**: assertiveness, interpersonal relationships, problem solving, happiness and empathy.

The good news was Amy scored high in both assertiveness and self-actualization, which would contribute to her goal of becoming a Star Performer. This same data shows she'd be more successful if she improved her empathy, interpersonal relationships and happiness scores and brought them into balance with assertiveness and self-actualization.

Amy gave an example of a recent appointment she had with a C-suite executive in charge of one of the billion-dollar petrochemical giants. In this meeting, she made some bold statements in presenting her research and recommendations, suggesting that her potential client could do better with his investments than he currently was. Amy even pointed out a calculation error the executive had made in his portfolio assumptions. Since the potential client held more academic credentials than Amy did, it was a stretch for her to voice such a strong opinion and afterward she was unsure of her behavior.

I reminded Amy her assertiveness score was considerably higher and out of balance with her self-regard. "That could contribute to your feeling of discomfort when asserting yourself," I said. "As you begin to feel more confidence in your skills from both a conscious and unconscious standpoint, you'll begin to feel surer of yourself and comfortable when making bold, direct statements."

We discussed ways she could learn to self-soothe her triggered emotions while also building self-regard. To do this, I suggested she use positive self-talk to keep affirming abundance – the idea that there are people out there who want and need her services, and want to find her as much as she wants to find them. When she repeated this affirmation daily, she relaxed and received more referrals from existing clients without even asking.

I also suggested she do research, reminding her that taking action and gathering information is a great antidote to anxiety, and ask her colleague who's always booked and overflowing with clients how she thinks and feels about her ability to attract new clients and grow her business. We decided to continue working on her optimism to strengthen her faith in her own abilities to attract new clients.

"What's the best way for me to connect with female clients?" Amy asked. I suggested once again working on empathy skills, specifically learning to listen attentively to what her female clients tell her, to build trust relationships.

"It would also help you to behave vulnerably and genuinely each time you meet with both new prospects and regular clients, specifically women," I advised.

Since Amy scored low in flexibility, she tended to behave rigidly in meetings with new prospects because she feared the unknown and didn't tolerate uncertainty well. By practicing feeling comfortable in the "not knowing," and having optimism about using a systematic, timeless referral process that works, she was able to slowly relax, loosen up and find more freedom in new situations. This had the added benefit of giving her more spontaneous access to her creativity, and she came up with numerous solutions to help new clients.

Another way we worked on increasing Amy's flexibility was to focus on those times when circumstances changed in the daily business environment, creating conditions that were out of her control and awkward for her. Since she didn't like change, she'd often react to interruptions in the workday by pounding on the vending machine to release packets of M&Ms. She called this "losing it."

Since she was frustrated with her lack of progress in this area, together we came up with a metric to measure it. We looked at the number of times she currently "lost it" – about five times a week for 15 minutes each episode. We decided to aim for reducing the frequency by one time each month until the behavior was eradicated. We also aimed to reduce the duration of the episode, stepping down the minutes incrementally for each episode in the same manner. That way, Amy could numerically track her progress, thereby developing her confidence.

To accomplish this, Amy had to learn new skills to calm herself when triggered by something unexpected. I taught her a deep breathing technique and how to use self-hypnosis. I suggested she continue using positive self-talk to make this change in her daily demeanor.

Eighth Consult

At this stage in the process, although Amy still didn't want to discuss her personal life, spontaneous memories of early childhood and negative experiences with her family began to surface for her. The uncomfortable memories surfaced whenever she was faced with emotional conflict involving other people: coworkers, clients, neighbors, acquaintances, friends, and her spouse and children.

Amy was very uncomfortable when caught in a situation that evoked any type of interpersonal conflict. In general, she handled it by getting angry and losing her temper. Because of her willingness to change, I persuaded her, though she was skeptical, to share with me what she was experiencing. As she told me story after story, she started to identify a negative pattern: She behaved with other people in ways her parents had behaved with her.

As a young girl, Amy hadn't liked some of the critical ways her parents had treated her and she had vowed to be different when she grew up. Despite this girlhood desire to change, she was following in their footsteps, and this was quite distressing to her. This type of unconscious pattern is actually normal and part of the human experience.

I spent a lot of time educating Amy about the different aspects of the mind: the logical center, the emotional center and the instinctual, also known as the reptile brain. I explained in detail how the reptile brain performed a life-saving function in caveperson days, protecting us from saber-toothed tigers, literally keeping us alive.

Today, however, there are no saber-toothed tigers and this part of our brain doesn't know the difference between an emotional threat and a physical one – and it definitely overreacts. This is the aspect of the mind that causes fight-or-flight syndrome, the adrenaline-cortisol rush that kicks us into emotional overdrive when we're triggered by upsetting events

Of course, it isn't the event or circumstance itself that triggers this response; rather, it's our interpretation or perception of the event controlling us in the moment. Some of our interpretations are accurate and some are irrational. The majority of the irrational thoughts and perceptions were put in place when we were quite young, when our brains weren't yet fully formed or developed. Yet it's these irrational thoughts that are triggered during upsetting events, so we're being guided as adults by decisions we made as children.

Daniel Goleman actually coined the term "emotional hijack" to describe how our rational/logical brain isn't able to respond when the instinctual or reptile brain has taken over and overwhelmed us. When this happens, we aren't thinking logically and we behave instinctively. Sadly, this is when we're most apt to make mistakes in our thinking, reality testing and impulse control, and it can have detrimental effects on our interpersonal relationships. And yet curiously, this is the moment when we have the best opportunity to create a positive change and raise our emotional intelligence.

In graduate school, I wrote a research paper on addictions and the concept of free-will choice. During my research, I discovered a book called *Shadow Syndromes: Discover the Hidden Time Bombs in Your Personality* by John J. Ratey. I was fascinated by the research that posited that even people whose brains have been habitually addicted to physical substances and other behaviors still had a chance to change.

The authors proposed that there's a 30-second span of time during which a person can exercise free will and change his or her thoughts and make a conscious choice, free of habitual thought patterns. The trick to this is to significantly slow down the thought process in the pivotal moment when the brain is being hijacked by irrational thoughts from the past. I was so excited to learn this because it gave me much hope: There's always a chance to think differently, and to change and choose new behaviors. We can always renew our minds.

I explained this research to Amy. She saw this type of unconscious pattern was controlling her daily behavior and agreed to face it head on. She agreed to write down every episode of conflict in her journal and to share it with me so I could help her learn from it and find a new behavior in similar situations as they arose.

Over time this helped her to become aware of situations that triggered her anger and the emotions that were underneath, such as fear, sadness, guilt, shame and embarrassment. These emotions sprang from childhood judgments that were no longer accurate predictors of current circumstances. They had to be examined and looked at from a new and healthier, more constructive perspective.

Amy learned to reframe old judgments and empower herself to look at her life from a fresh perspective. It's just like when an old vinyl LP gets scratched and the needle gets stuck in the scratch instead of the groove. It can't move backward or forward, the music repeating over and over again. This was my analogy for how Amy's brain was stuck in the scratch, causing bothersome repeats that prevented her from moving forward.

The work we did together was the equivalent of lifting the needle and placing it in the proper groove. Then Amy could take charge of her own decisions again and be better able to make choices that integrated both emotion and logic. A great benefit was the concomitant increase in Amy's stress tolerance skills.

Another behavior limiting Amy was her addiction to caffeine and sugar, primarily energy drinks and M&Ms. We both thought the large amounts of energy drinks she consumed daily contributed to her anxiety, and her inability to self-soothe and handle stress. This was also likely keeping her awake at night, interfering with refreshing and restful sleep.

"I consume the energy drinks to give myself a boost," Amy told me. "I eat handfuls of M&Ms throughout the day and that calms me down."

I suggested in reality, consuming excessive caffeine and sugar actually exacerbated her anxiety. I asked Amy to start slowly cutting back the number of energy drinks she drank, replacing them with water. She also began limiting her sugar consumption, allowing herself a few M&Ms only at certain intervals during the day, eventually dropping the habit entirely.

Amy was dubious because the caffeinated drinks and sugar formed a ritual for her, a comforting part of her daily routine. "People with anxiety and control issues cling to routines because the routines are predictable and reassuring," I explained. "After 9/11, there were many articles written encouraging people to return to their daily routines, sticking to them as much as possible to regain a sense of normality. Of course, some routines are healthy and some aren't. The unhealthy ones need to be changed."

I encouraged Amy to review her daily routines to discern which ones were healthful and which were not. One of the things we discovered was that her routines were too rigid and boxed her in, including eating the same thing for breakfast and lunch every day.

This type of behavior is too stifling to one's creativity so I encouraged her to change it up a bit. I suggested trying a new food for breakfast one day a week for a sense of novelty and adventure. Trying new things stimulates our thinking and builds new neurological pathways in the brain, providing a sense of excitement, a wonderful antidote to combat the effects of stress.

As Amy experimented with new ways of eating and drinking, she was amazed at how much better she felt. She continued to examine her habits, adding exciting new components to her daily schedule and dropping boring, worn-out activities from her routine.

Ninth Consult

At this meeting Amy was still concerned about how quickly she could become angry, react negatively with a client, and then wish she hadn't.

She was still plagued by uncertainty about how to prioritize and use her time effectively, and she wanted me to tell her what to do. I suggested her lack of impulse control could be related to symptoms of burnout; for example, she didn't like to take time off from work. This was a function of her anxiety: The possibility of failing to reach her production goals kept her at the office for long hours, far past the point of being efficient and genuinely productive.

I suggested Amy make a commitment and set an intention to figure out how to spend her time. I told her to relax and allow her inner wisdom to give her the answers she sought, letting her gut feelings guide the way. Essentially, she could sit down and imagine herself doing certain tasks in her mind's eye, paying attention to the feelings that arose in her imagination as she visualized herself completing the tasks. In this way, her own inner wisdom could tell her which things to do first and which things to let go of based on the type of feelings that were generated, either a sense of accomplishment or of wasted time.

One of my goals from the start had been to help Amy build a sense of inner direction and guidance, or independence, rather than depending on me to tell her what to do or how to manage her career. As she built trust in her own ability to figure out the solution (that's stress tolerance) she could remain calm in the face of challenges, her inner creativity guiding her in the best direction.

It made sense to me that Amy felt burned out. She'd been juggling a lot of stress at home and at work for a long time. She was like a lot of people who, when they feel hungry, angry, lonely, or tired (H-A-L-T) simultaneously, they feel hopeless. When they build their stress tolerance, they develop a more positive response to external stimuli; they can tell themselves that as long as they control their ability to calm down, everything will work out. It's empowering to have the feeling that you can control or influence a stressful situation by staying calm and monitoring your emotions.

One way Amy could regain control over the triggering effects of her reptile brain was by using a cognitive behavioral restructuring exercise. The idea is to identify triggers for the most common negative thoughts or negative self-talk and then debunk them, much like defusing a ticking time bomb. These thoughts can then be reframed and changed into positive affirmations. When done consistently, you can put the brakes on your negative self-talk and become a positive cheerleader for yourself instead. I shared with Amy the ABCDE exercise, taught to me by my mentor, Dr. Dana Ackley, specifically for this type of reframing. (See the back of this book for details on how to use this method.)

At this meeting, Amy again mentioned her recurring fear that when her schedule wasn't full of appointments, she worried about how she'd find her next new client. She worried that her production would dip and her business wouldn't be sustainable. Although her concern was valid because changes in today's business climate are fast and furious and can come from any direction, the probability of her going out of business was very slim. Her fears were driving her to overreact and imagine the worst possible outcome.

In fact, Amy's best chance of building her client base was to take action in the face of fear and do things to strengthen her own optimism. Stronger optimism skills serve as a motivator so she could continue taking action and advancing her strategic plan. Her best chance of retaining her client base was to grow her interpersonal relationships skills since clients these days want to work with providers they trust and whose opinion they value.

I suggested to Amy that during days or weeks such as this, she should look at her to-do list and use the unscheduled time to work down the list. She could also engage in other activities to strengthen her ability to attract new, ideal clients, such as studying and researching prospecting, business development or marketing; updating her website; or reviewing her business plan.

She needed to understand unscheduled time is as important as time scheduled for client meetings. This again is the concept of working on the business vs. working in the business. Both are equally important activities, so I encouraged Amy to stay focused and intentional about her activities.

Tenth and Eleventh Consults

The majority of time during these two meetings was devoted to discussing recent events in Amy's personal life. They had a common theme: All the events and situations had activated her hurt and had triggered drawer-slamming anger. Each time she had reacted from the reptile brain despite her best efforts. Although she attempted to run through the ABCDE exercise I had taught her (see the back of the book), she initially had trouble executing it and getting to a place of a calm mind.

This is to be expected since the exercise takes practice and repetition to achieve optimal results. Amy walked me through each of the troubling family situations and together we used the ABCDE exercise to explore and identify irrational beliefs that contributed to her less-than-optimal behaviors.

During these discussions, we needed to address guilt and shame from events in Amy's past. I define guilt and shame this way: Guilt is doing something wrong, and shame is thinking you're a bad person. I wanted to help her see that while she had made some wrong choices in the past, she was still a good person at the core. Alleviating guilt and shame helps build self-regard. Said another way, it's important to accept your weaknesses as well as your strengths without shame to be able to build self-confidence.

Twelfth Consult and Conclusion

This meeting came at year-end, so we took the opportunity to look back at Amy's original goals and the developmental emotional intelligence plan I had created, so we could assess her progress. Here's the direct feedback I offered on her progress towards her original goals:

- **To be authentic and follow your own path to success**. Since you understand where your emotions and behaviors come from, you're behaving in more authentic ways that allow you to better connect with people. This is helping you convert more prospects to clients.

- **To figure out who you are so you can approach work your own way, without having to model other people's approaches**. By learning to ask for help, being less independent and more collaborative, you're finding your own style when asking for referrals. You're consistently generating more referrals.

- **To "win" at work and know you do a really good job**. You're starting to evaluate your progress holistically: You're not just looking at dollars earned and production measures to judge your overall success. Instead, you're also including the positive behaviors you're repeating on a consistent basis to keep moving forward on your goals. You recognize this as part of the bigger picture of maintaining a viable business. This is increasing your self-regard.

- **To have no regrets**. The work we've done to help clear shame and guilt has helped you feel that instead of regrets, you've learned a lot from your life experiences. You've reframed your regrets as grist for the mill: What you've learned from past mistakes helps you move forward now in a way that deepens your relationships with those around you.

- **To comfortably set expectations when working with clients**. Since we worked on your client-approach language, you're more adept at assessing their needs and expressing your own. As a result, you have a better working relationship with your ideal clients. You're using your assertiveness skills in a more meaningful way.

- **To know when you have influence with another person**. Because we worked on your emotional self-awareness, you sense when you're relating well with clients, prospects, staff, and family and friends. When you aren't, you're able to monitor your reactions and adjust accordingly.

- **To position yourself as an expert in your field**. Because we worked on your authenticity, you're better able to position yourself as a subject matter expert without coming across as a pushy salesperson. We worked on your branding so you feel it presents a professional and genuine image of you and your way of working with clients.

- **To identify your target market and ideal client profile**. You've identified your target market and mapped out your ideal client profile to your satisfaction. You're attracting more clients in your target market who are consistent with your planned ideals. This is decreasing your anxiety and increasing your happiness.

In terms of the emotional intelligence skills development plan, Amy made improvements in the five skills we originally identified: self-regard, emotional self-awareness, empathy, flexibility and reality testing. In addition, she said she was becoming a happier person and reported experiencing a greater sense of well-being. She made the greatest improvement in the two skills that serve as a foundation for the rest of the emotional intelligence skills: self-regard and emotional self-awareness, which was the best possible outcome as a result of our work together.

I noted these positive things Amy had in her favor:

- She was already more successful than others in her industry.

- She was a seasoned professional who had perseverance and staying power.

- She was smart and had the ability to accumulate high-caliber certifications and credentials to position her as an expert.

- She has a sense of humor that helps others connect with her. We still had a lot of work to do in the areas of empathy and optimism. I suggested we continue working together to build her empathy, which would help her better relate to people, especially female clients and also to develop a more positive attitude that would sustain her creativity and focus during leaner times. I also suggested Amy practice these skills by learning to relate to me in a more generous, reciprocal manner.

I specifically challenged her to let go of her resistance and give serious thought to some of my questions, allowing us to dig deeper into some of her more sensitive topic areas. In this case, I felt Amy had increased her self-regard and emotional self-awareness to a point where we were ready for the next step.

During the second year we worked together, Amy was more engaged and willing to dive deeper into identifying and reframing her irrational thoughts. While it was an intense year of work for her, she made great progress. In the end, we agreed she had dramatically transformed negative residue from a chaotic childhood and earned a positive sense of herself.

She accepted both the worst and the best parts of her personality, which meant she judged herself and others a lot less than previously. Because of this change, she was also more flexible and vulnerable in her presentation to others. As a result, her clients felt she related to them in a more genuine way, to the point where they knew she really cared about them. She became more authentic.

Today Amy is more self-accepting, relaxed, easygoing and happy. Her personal definition of success has changed from accumulation of wealth and exceeding high expectations to helping others, having fun and earning money along the way. She's happy and successful, and reports having a greater quality of daily life, too. "All the hard work I had to do in our coaching was a worthwhile investment that paid off in spades," she told me.

Conclusion

Would you agree now that emotional intelligence is key to your personal and professional success?

Since the 1990s, Multi-Health Systems, together with a global network of researchers and practitioners, has administered the EQ-i and the EQ-i 2.0, which has been translated into 45 languages, to more than 1 million people in 66 countries.

"This has built up a voluminous data bank and uncovering incontrovertible links between emotional intelligence and proven success in people's personal and working lives. Based on our findings, we know beyond doubt that EQ can be accurately determined and effectively improved upon on an individual basis," wrote Steven J. Stein, Ph.D., and Howard E. Book, M.D., in their book, *The EQ Edge: Emotional Intelligence and Your Success.*

Companies and organizations that integrate emotional intelligence in at least two different ways are 25% more likely to have "extremely effective" leadership development, wrote Dr. Steven Stein in his book, *The EQ Leader: Instilling Passion, Creating Shared Goals, and Building Meaningful Organizations Through Emotional Intelligence.* Contrast that with only 15% of firms that don't implement EQ training and report effective leadership development.

"Incorporating emotional intelligence as part of leadership coaching supports higher performance," Dr. Stein wrote. "When organizations incorporate emotional intelligence in leadership coaching, they are 36% more likely to report effective emotional intelligence training performance."

Our workplaces are filled with people who possess different personalities, strengths and emotions, which all influence the way they perform.

As you've learned, emotional intelligence (EQ) is our ability to identify and manage our (and other people's) emotions. EQ is a key indicator in predicting human performance and development potential, and encompasses a set of learnable skills that we can target and evolve over time. One reason the research is so promising is because it shows that anyone, at any age, can increase their EQ. Unlike IQ, EQ isn't static over time.

High EQ directly correlates to high productivity and profitability, as well as success and happiness.

While working in my therapy practice for more than 16 years, I observed that the skills leading to positive personal relationships are the same, exact ones required to achieve workplace success. I'm trained to work with clients systemically and holistically. I help them resolve irrational thoughts (from early childhood and personal issues) that negatively affect professional relationships. Together we correct workplace behaviors that keep them from achieving their full potential. This perspective helps my clients achieve long-lasting mindset and behavioral shifts that benefit them personally and professionally.

It's really crucial for managers and other business leaders to operate in emotionally intelligent ways to meet the needs of today's employees, and also to model those behaviors for their team. If you're ready to take the first step to increasing your workplace's EQ, you can:

- Learn more from your team and communicate better, increasing overall efficiency and morale

- Grow a playful, productive workplace with effective communication

- Increase your operational efficiency and quality through collaborative teamwork

- Increase your sales through emotionally intelligent sales reps

- Shorten sales cycles so your reps can close more deals.

I shared with you that I used to be so poor at managing my emotions that I cried during results reviews because I wasn't able to tolerate negative feedback. It's not that I was incompetent, it's just that I inherited negative belief patterns from the environment I grew up in. Convinced I could overcome this, I found help to improve my EQ and got hooked on studying what makes people happy and successful both at work and at home.

When you're my client, I listen carefully to what's keeping you up at night in regards to running your business, managing your career and your team, or building relationships in your personal life. I help you identify thoughts and emotions that hold you back from achieving your goals. We engage in dynamic discussions to help you imagine what you want your future to look like, and together we work to execute your vision.

When there's clarity of vision, thoughts, emotions and focus, you have the motivation and fortitude to achieve your goals. To begin, I do a thorough assessment of your situation, either by interviewing you and relevant team members or by using several proven assessment tools, including the EQ-i 2.0. Once we know your emotional strengths and behavioral weaknesses we create a developmental plan to help you balance them and increase your EQ.

If you're a leader, to optimize your performance, we also focus on the Four Pillars of Leadership in the EQ-i 2.0 model: authenticity, coaching, insight and innovation. These four pillars are invaluable in bolstering your leadership style and positioning you most favorably to lead an effective team. We also examine your Leadership Derailers, the factors that research has been shown to be most indicative of leadership failure. Four subscales are emphasized in the EQ-i leadership report because of their stronger correlation to leadership failure: impulse control, stress tolerance, problem solving and independence.

Finally, we focus on building the EQ skills known to predict success in your industry. Together we increase your EQ while improving performance, productivity and profitability. This makes you more successful and happy, across a variety of different contexts, both at home and at work. I know the process works because it worked for me and for so many of my clients, to whom I'm grateful for staying open-minded to the beneficial power of increasing their emotional intelligence.

To learn more or get started, visit www.eqicoach.com, for individual as well as corporate leadership and EQ programs.

The Bar-On Facets of EQ-i 2.0: 16 Skills Definitions

Self-Regard: the ability to respect and accept yourself as basically good.

Self-Actualization: the ability to realize your potential capacities.

Emotional Self-Awareness: the ability to accurately recognize your feelings.

Emotional Expression: the ability to express your feelings verbally and non-verbally.

Independence: the ability to be self-directed and self-controlled in your thinking and actions and be free of emotional dependency.

Assertiveness: the ability to express feelings, beliefs, and thoughts, and defend your rights in a nondestructive manner.

Interpersonal Relationships: the ability to establish and maintain mutually satisfying relationships characterized by intimacy and by giving and receiving affection.

Empathy: the ability to be aware of, understand and appreciate others' feelings.

Social Responsibility: the ability to be a cooperative, contributing and constructive member of your social group.

Problem Solving: the ability to identify and define problems as well as to generate and implement potentially effective solutions.

Reality Testing: the ability to assess the correspondence between what you experience and what objectively exists.

Impulse Control: the ability to resist or delay an impulse, drive, or temptation to act.

Stress Tolerance: the ability to withstand adverse events and stressful situations without "falling apart" by actively and positively coping with stress.

Flexibility: the ability to adjust your emotions, thoughts and behavior to changing situations and conditions.

Optimism: the ability to look at the brighter side of life and to maintain a positive attitude, even in the face of adversity (a focus on the future).

Happiness: the ability to feel satisfied with your life, to enjoy yourself and others, and to have fun (a focus on the present).

The Four Pillars of Leadership in the EQ-i 2.0 Model

Authenticity: The ability to be an inspiring role model, and displaying fair and moral behavior.

Coaching: Operating as a mentor, supporting your employees' needs.

Insight: Communicating with a purpose, meaning, and vision.

Innovation: Spurring ingenuity, imagination and autonomous thinking.

The ABCDE Method and Example

I've referenced the ABCDE exercise in several chapters. This is an analytical method developed by Dr. Albert Ellis (for more information, read "Rational-emotive therapy" by Albert Ellis in *Theoretical and empirical foundations of rational-emotive therapy* edited by Albert J. Ellis and J.M. Whiteley).

I learned about this method from my mentor coach, Dr. Dana Ackley. It's a way to identify and change irrational thought patterns that are commonly a root cause of excess emotion. (For a more detailed explanation of this process read *The EQ Edge: Emotional Intelligence and Your Success, Revised & Updated*, by Steven J. Stein, Ph.D. and Howard E. Book, M.D.)

We all have irrational thoughts, because we're human. Irrational thoughts are born in early childhood, when we try to take in the adult world around us and make sense of it with a child's immature brain. Because our minds aren't fully formed when we're children, we can't accurately assess the world around us so we make up childlike stories to explain what we see. This behavior helps us survive childhood, but

EQ-i 2.0 Skills Definitions

it doesn't serve us in adulthood. As if on autopilot though, we still use these ingrained childhood explanations to help us make sense of things as adults, only they don't work. We end up getting triggered and emotionally hijacked because we forget to go back and update our foregone conclusions.

Another way we learn irrational thought patterns and then adopt them is through watching our parents, teachers and other trusted authority figures. Although they mean well, they may be trapped in their own unconscious thoughts that they pass along to us.

Irrational thought patterns can develop in adulthood, in three different ways:

1. Going through an emotionally traumatic experience often leaves irrational residue (hearing sirens may trigger memories of being in an ambulance).

2. Most company cultures include irrational ways of thinking ("Success demands that we consistently work overtime!"). Daily exposure to such culturally-based irrational thinking can lead us to adopt it without noticing we're doing so.

3. The national culture shares a number of widely held irrational beliefs:

   - "Wealthy people are happier."
   - "Successful people have no problems."
   - "Blondes are more attractive."

One way to regain control over the triggering effects of the primitive reptile brain is by using a cognitive behavioral restructuring exercise. The idea is to identify the triggers for your most common negative thoughts or negative self-talk and then debunk them, sort of like defusing a ticking time bomb. Then, reframe them and change them into positive affirmations. When you practice this consistently, you can put the brakes on your negative self-talk and become a positive cheerleader for yourself instead.

The ABCDE exercise is a way of gaining conscious control over our thinking, which can help build new neural pathways relevant to the emotional intelligence factor under development.

The letters are an acronym designed to help you remember the sequence of events to study:

A: Activating Event

B: Belief

C: Consequence

D: Debate and Dispute (the belief)

E: Emotional Effect (of debate and dispute)

Let's apply this example to a financial advisor who's struggling with Impulse Control and wants to build his patience. We'll go through this exercise as if you're the advisor.

"A" stands for the Activating Event that triggers the reptile brain response. Your client calls five minutes before your meeting, and says she can't make it without giving an understandable reason for the last-minute change. Let's assume you spent four hours preparing for the meeting, drafting recommendations for her investment portfolio and re-hearsing the meeting in your mind. Even if she reschedules, you've wasted time because you will have to re-prepare (our brains don't re-member every detail of the case material indefinitely) for the rescheduled meeting.

Again, since you don't know the reason for the last-minute schedule change, it might be hard to access your empathy skills.

"B" stands for Belief. You might assume the client doesn't value your time, is uninterested in what you've prepared, is never going to meet with you again and you're going to lose her business. In fact, all your clients may suddenly cancel and you might lose all your business, so you're surely going to fail! You might even have to start planning to switch careers right now. The reptile brain leads us down irrational paths such as these.

"C" stands for Consequence. This belief hurts and you react by getting angry while you're still on the phone with the client. Your reptile brain perceives danger (albeit, emotional in nature only) and focuses on every time anyone ever cancelled on you with late notice, was a no-show or gave you the impression they devalued your time. This focus could reinforce an irrational thought pattern and elicit even greater anger. You're now in a bind and in danger of saying something you'll regret later.

"D" stands for Debate and Dispute. As you feel your emotions ramping up, you can choose to stop yourself before you endanger the long-term client relationship in one second flat.

EQ-i 2.0 Skills Definitions

Just in time to prevent yourself from an awkward moment, you can take a deep breath and quickly run through this series of questions designed to help you think rationally:

- **"Where's the proof?"** You might ask yourself if the client cancels every meeting and this is a predictable pattern of behavior or if this is a rare, one-time event.

- **"Are there alternative, more logical explanations for the activating event?"** What else might explain the client's behavior? Is it possible she has an emergency and doesn't wish to share that information with you for privacy reasons or maybe she's in a hurry to take care of it?

- **"If this happened to a colleague, and he asked for my advice, what would I tell him to help him look at it differently?"** Asking yourself this question will give you some emotional distance from the event and you might be able to detach from your anger and defuse it.

- **"Have I ever been in a similar situation before, had similar beliefs, and then discovered I was wrong?"** Ask yourself if you have a pattern of expecting the worst possible outcome because your anxiety fuels your fear of failure. Perhaps you jump to the wrong conclusions because this fear is so prevalent it unconsciously controls your every move.

- **"If I've been in this situation before, what have I learned that I can apply now?"** Upon reflection, you might remember a time when this happened before and you found out later the client had to rush his mother to the hospital and couldn't tell you until the next meeting. Perhaps it's better to give him the benefit of the doubt, be patient and wait to see what happens next. Many things have a way of working themselves out if we're patient and curious.

"E" stands for Emotional Effect. Running through these questions and disputing your irrational thoughts is likely to calm your hurt and anger down to an appropriate level of concern. When you're hurt and angry you won't be able to sort things through clearly and chances are you won't make good decisions. When you're in a calmer state, though circumstances might not be optimal, you'll be in a better position to ask meaningful questions and sort out a mutually acceptable solution. The paradox for many people who've been ignoring emotional data in favor of their intellect is that by allowing yourself to focus on emotions, you actually gain more control over your intellect.

The combination of irrational thought plus excessive emotion can be described as a low emotional intelligence strategy (remember Stacy in the Self-Expression Composite?). In fact, a low emotional intelligence factor is often at the root of one or more patterns of irrational thought. Going through an ABCDE analysis will help you think more effectively and contain your emotion to a manageable intensity. As a result, you'll be better able to identify superior behavioral alternatives within the target situation.

Use this exercise the next time you're having an emotional response to an event in your personal or professional life. Jot down notes next to each of the letters to help you work through your best response.

A: Activating Event

B: Belief

C: Consequence

D: Debate and Dispute

- Where's the proof?
- Are there alternative, more logical explanations for the activating event?
- If this happened to a colleague, and he asked for my advice, what would I tell him to help him look at it differently?
- Have I ever been in a similar situation before, had similar beliefs, and then discovered I was wrong?
- If I've been in this situation before, what have I learned that I can apply now?

E: Emotional Effect

Additional Resources

Books

Emotional Intelligence in Couples Therapy: Advances from Neurobiology and the Science of Intimate Relationships by Brent J. Atkinson. W. W. Norton & Company, New York. 2005.

The Handbook of Emotional Intelligence: Theory, Development, Assessment, and Application at Home, School, and in the Workplace edited by Reuven Bar-On and James D.A. Parker. Jossey-Bass, San Francisco. 2000.

The Hero's Journey by Joseph Campbell. Harpers, San Francisco. 2001.

The Five Love Languages: The Secret to Love that Lasts by Gary Chapman. Northfield Publishing, Plano, TX. (Reprint edition) 2015.

The Emotional Side of Organizations: Applications of Bowenian Theory edited by Patricia A. Comella, Joyce Bader, Judith S. Ball, Kathleen K. Wiseman and Ruth Riley Sagar. Georgetown Family Center, Washington, D.C. 2012.

The Handbook of Emotionally Intelligent Leadership: Inspiring Others to Achieve Results by Daniel Feldman, Ph.D. Leadership Performance Solutions Press. 1999.

Emotional Intelligence: Why It Can Matter More Than IQ by Daniel Goleman. Bantam Books, New York, 1995.

Primal Leadership: Unleashing the Power of Emotional Intelligence by Daniel Goleman, Annie McKee and Richard Boyatzis. Harvard Business Review Press, Boston. 2013.

Getting the Love You Want: A Guide for Couples by Harville Hendrix, Ph.D. Henry Holt & Co., New York. (Revised edition) 2007.

Emotional Intelligence in Action: Training and Coaching Activities for Leaders, Managers, and Teams by Marcia Hughes and James Tomford Terrell. Multi-Health Systems Inc., Canada. 2011.

Handbook for Developing Emotional and Social Intelligence: Best Practices, Case Studies, and Strategies by Marcia Hughes and Henry L. Thompson Ph.D. Pfeiffer, San Francisco. 2009.

Feel the Fear ... and Do It Anyway by Susan Jeffers. New York, Ballantine Books. (20th anniversary edition) 2006.

On Death and Dying: What the Dying Have to Teach Doctors, Nurses, Clergy and Their Own Families by Dr. Elizabeth Kubler-Ross. New York, Scribner. (Reprint edition) 2014.

Becoming a Resonant Leader: Develop Your Emotional Intelligence, Renew Your Relationships, Sustain Your Effectiveness by Annie McKee, Richard Boyatzis and Frances Johnston. Harvard Business Review Press, Boston. 2008.

The Paradox of Success: When Winning at Work Means Losing at Life by John R. O'Neil. Tarcher Master Mind Editions. Penguin Books, New York. 1993. 2004.

Introduction to Type and Emotional Intelligence: Pathways to Performance by Roger R. Pearman. CPP, Palo Alto, CA. 2002.

Winning in the Trust and Value Economy: A Guide to Sales Success and Business Growth by Meridith Elliott Powell. Global Professional Publishing. 2013.

Shadow Syndromes: Discover the Hidden Time Bombs in Your Personality by John J. Ratey, M.D.

Understanding Organizations: Applications of Bowen Family Systems Theory edited by Ruth Riley Sagar and Kathleen Klaus Wiseman. Georgetown Family Center, Washington, D.C. 2012.

The EQ Edge: Emotional Intelligence and Your Success, Revised & Updated by Steven J. Stein, Ph.D. and Howard E. Book, M.D. Jossey-Bass, Canada. (Third edition) 2011.

The EQ Leader: Instilling Passion, Creating Shared Goals, and Building Meaningful Organizations Through Emotional Intelligence by Steven J. Stein, Ph.D. Wiley, Hoboken, NJ. (First edition) 2017.

Trust Your Life: Forgive Yourself and Go After Your Dreams by Noelle Sterne. Unity, 2011.

True Work: Doing What You Love and Loving What You Do by Justine and Michael Toms. Easton, PA, Harmony. 1999.

Emotional Intelligence: A Practical Guide by Dr. Dustin Walton. MJF Books, New York. 2012.

Online Resources

The Center for Creative Leadership: www.ccl.org

The EI Consortium: www.eiconsortium.org

The Hay Group: www.haygroup.com

The Human Capital Institute: www.hci.org

Leadership Performance Solutions: www.leadershipperformance.com

Xcellero Leadership: xcellero.com

Emotional Intelligence Thought Leaders:

Dr. Dana Ackley: www.eqleader.net

Dr. Reuven Bar-On: www.reuvenbaron.org

Richard Boyatzis: http://bit.ly/2DDyYrK

Dr. Daniel Goleman: www.danielgoleman.info

Collaborative Growth's Marcia Hughes & James Terrell: www.cgrowth.com

Annie McKee: bit.ly/2rdmhkJ

Index

About the Author

An accomplished business executive and licensed therapist, **Roberta Ann Moore** helps busy C-suiters and rising corporate stars balance financial and business demands with their important personal relationships.

Her mission is to help people understand that healthy relationships start by setting boundaries, as well as developing strong emotional intelligence and interpersonal relationship skills like empathy, that will work for you in the office and at home.

While working in her therapy practice, Moore observed that the skills leading to successful personal relationships are the same ones we need to achieve workplace success. With this discovery, Moore became certified in Dr. Reuven Bar-On's Model of Emotional Intelligence, and launched Moore Relationships.

Moore blended lessons she learned during her 18-year accounting and banking career, and over 16 years of systems-based psychotherapy practice, to specialize in helping executives, business teams and sales teams achieve personal and workplace success. Moore believes all corporate performance is created by superior execution.

That means improving emotional intelligence skills has a direct impact upon how professionals execute strategic plans and create results. Better 'people skills' allows executives and managers to influence their employees and peers to take their organizations to the next level.

Every day, Moore helps corporate teams, executives, entrepreneurs and other leaders who work for startups, nonprofits, small and mid-sized businesses, and large corporations succeed through improved emotional, social and cognitive intelligence behaviors and skills. She provides emotional intelligence assessments, training and development using the EQ-i 2.0 and EQ 360 programs as a framework.

Continue Your Emotional Intelligence Journey

Looking for an engaging and meaningful way to develop your emotional intelligence?

For over 16 years, Roberta Moore has been helping people develop the 16 skills in Dr. Reuven Bar-On's model, the EQ-i 2.0. If the way Ms. Moore worked with the client characters resonated with you, contact her to learn how she can work with you or your company.

Visit www.eqicoach.com to:

1. Ready to take an assessment to learn about your emotional intelligence?

2. Ready for coaching that will transform your career and life?

3. Want to book Ms. Moore for a fun, informative speaking engagement or workshop?

4. Want to order more books for your group or company?

5. Want to sign up for Ms. Moore's blog?

Connect with Roberta Moore via LinkedIn:

Linkedin.com/in/robertamoore

Moore Relationships offers a variety of different coaching and consulting services including: leadership and talent development, executive coaching, group coaching and team development, and sales acceleration coaching. In addition, she is qualified to use the following assessments: EQ-i 2.0, Everything DiSC and Myers-Briggs (MBTI) Personality Indicator. Roberta Moore is available for keynote workshops and other speaking engagements.

For a complete list of possible workshop topics, please consult her website: www.eqicoach.com.

51635989R00133

Made in the USA
Columbia, SC
22 February 2019